THE SEVEN DEADLY SINS

Other books by Kevin Vost
from Sophia Institute Press:

Memorize the Faith!
Fit for Eternal Life!
The One-Minute Aquinas
Unearthing Your Ten Talents

KEVIN VOST, PSY.D.

THE
SEVEN
DEADLY
SINS

A THOMISTIC GUIDE TO
VANQUISHING VICE AND SIN

SOPHIA INSTITUTE PRESS
Manchester, New Hampshire

Sophia Institute Press
Box 5284, Manchester, NH 03108
1-800-888-9344

www.SophiaInstitute.com

Sophia Institute Press® is a registered trademark of Sophia Institute.

Library of Congress Cataloging-in-Publication Data

Vost, Kevin.
    The seven deadly sins (and their forty-four death-dealing daughters) : a Thomistic guide to vanquishing vice and sin / Kevin Vost, Psy.D.
        pages cm
    Includes bibliographical references.
    ISBN 978-1-62282-234-8 (pbk. : alk. paper) 1. Deadly sins. I. Title.
    BV4626.V67 2015
    241'.3 — dc23

                                            2014044561

To Eloisa Eryn Basuel Vost

"Grandchildren are the crown of the aged."
(Proverbs 17:6)

Contents

Foreword

For the past six years I have had the tremendous pleasure of count-ing Kevin Vost among my closest friends. I met Kevin shortly after reading—and, I must add, greatly benefiting from—his books *Memorize the Faith!* and *Fit for Eternal Life!* Since that time I have had the good fortune of enjoying countless conversations, collaborating with him on a book and a monthly radio program, and studying each of his subsequent books.

Proverbs 27:17 tells us, "Iron sharpens iron, and one man sharpens another." Let me assure you: men do not come any sharper than Dr. Kevin Vost. Kevin has so fully assimilated the thought of St. Thomas Aquinas and his massive *Summa Theo-logica* that he is able to articulate it in the words of today's man and woman in the pew.

That you have opened this particular book by Dr. Vost means that you recognize the destructive power of sin and want to understand its insidious nature and begin the serious work of beating back its power in your life. *The Seven Deadly Sins* will help you do precisely that. Not only does this book present you with the insights of St. Thomas, who seemed to have synthesized the thought of all the great philosophers and theologians who preceded him, but it unites them with the insights of Kevin as a doctor of psychology. Most importantly, however, it takes seri-ously the New Testament's claims that all growth in virtue is the result of Christ's grace and that we must do all in our power to cooperate with that grace (Phil. 2:12–13).

By the time you've finished this book you will have set out anew on the path to heaven. Your gaze will be sharper, your ability to evaluate the spiritual terrain more pronounced; and as a result, your steps will be more deliberate. You will have been led through a penetrating examination of conscience, given practical steps to squash vice and cultivate virtue, and directed to the powerful channels of grace that Christ entrusted to the Church. And I have no doubt that, like me, you will recognize Dr. Kevin Vost as one of today's most gifted communicators of the Church's divine and timeless wisdom.

—Shane Kapler
St. Louis, Missouri
October 1, 2014
Feast of St. Thérèse of Lisieux

Acknowledgments

Many thanks once again to Charlie McKinney, Aja McCarthy, Carolyn McKinney, Nora Malone, Sheila Perry, and all at Sophia Institute Press for bringing another of my titles to print just a year or so after the last one. Any literary sloth I might have harbored in my heart was clearly no match for the inspiration, encouragement, good counsel, and plain old hard work they provided.

THE SEVEN DEADLY SINS

The World's Deadliest Sins

For the wages of sin is death, but the free gift of
God is eternal life in Christ Jesus our Lord.

—ROMANS 6:23

No man can be the sufficient cause of another's
spiritual death, because no man dies spiritually except by sinning of his own will.

—ST. THOMAS AQUINAS

ST, I-II, Q. 73, ART. 8

What Is the Deadliest Sin in the World?

What is the *world's deadliest sin*? This may not be the easiest question to answer. It's not like trying to find out the *world's deadliest joke*. The Monty Python crew took that on in the 1960s in their comical skit "The World's Funniest Joke." They didn't reveal just what the joke was, not in English anyway, but as the story went, the joke, apparently written in the 1940s, was so funny that it was *deadly*. Indeed, it proved lethal to the joke's own author and to the police officers investigating his death. Any who chanced upon it and read or heard it would fall to their death amid uncontrollable convulsions of laughter. A team of British military experts translated it into German,[1] whence it was used as an effective weapon against the Nazis. And as the farcical story ends, at the end of World War II it was forever buried for the safety of mankind.

Now, we know that jokes aren't *really* deadly. Side-splitting jokes don't really split our sides. What then do jokes have to do with deadly sins? This introduction is not really about deadly or even sinful *jokes* but about *sins* that really can be

---

[1] How did the translators survive it? Reportedly, each translator was given only *one word* of the joke, and indeed, an unfortunate man who saw *two words* ended up spending two weeks in the hospital!

5

deadly to our souls. Unfortunately, these are the kinds of sins the modern world may joke about, considering them things that enlightened, secular, "post-Christian" people should not seriously consider sinful. Some even champion them as very *good things* indeed.

- *Sloth?* "Get real. Work smarter, not harder." Laziness is a sin? "If Christian Tradition is to be believed, the simple act of laziness can send you to hell!"[2] (Suggesting, perhaps, that it's a good thing we are "post-Christian"!)

- Isn't *envy* good for the causes of equality and social justice? Why shouldn't we be sad when others are richer than we are and have things that we don't? Why shouldn't we be happy if they lose their wealth or have it taken against their will?

- What's wrong with *avarice?* The one who dies with the most toys wins, right? Remember that line from the *Wall Street* movie proclaiming that "greed is good"?

- *Vainglory?* Where would we be without *pride?* We've all heard of Black pride, gay pride, school pride, team pride, and what student should not be taught to develop high self-esteem?

- When was the last time you heard a homily on *gluttony?* "Supersize mine, please — and hurry! I've got to get home to watch the Food Channel (or is it Network?)."

---

[2] This is the last line of a History Channel documentary on the sin of sloth in their series *Seven Deadly Sins,* DVD released April 28, 2009. We'll examine this statement's accuracy in chapter 8, "Slashing Sloth."

- How old-fashioned to think that *lust* is a sin, when we've been told for over fifty years, "If it feels good, do it!" Aren't we finally sexually liberated, after all?

- And tell me, what's wrong with *wrath*? "Nice guys finish last!" Shouldn't mothers be "MADD" against drunk drivers? Are we to become a nation of wimps?

Many modern takes on the very ancient concept of "deadly sins" are quite muddled, to say the least, laden with falsehoods, misunderstandings, and half-truths that can lead us away from Him who is the Truth with a capital T, and the way and the life as well.[3] Are there times when the "deadly sins" really are *good* for us? Are these sins merely *feelings*? Do we really need the old-fashioned notion of sin, let alone that dusty-old "medieval" list of seven deadly sins that "aren't in the Bible, anyway"?

We'll argue in the pages ahead that these sins can truly be deadly, and that one of them can truly be called *the deadliest sin in the world*. If you don't know it, I'm not going to spoil it for you in this introduction. We'll see down the road how the virtue of *patience* is one of the remedies to one of the top contenders (i.e., *wrath*), so let's exercise a little patience now, since I need to explain what I mean by a "Thomistic approach" to the seven deadly sins.

Why a "Thomistic Approach"?

The *Thom* in *Thomistic* refers to St. Thomas Aquinas (1225–1274), the great medieval theologian and Doctor of the Catholic

---

[3] *"Via, Veritas, Vita,"* if you'd care for the pithy alliterative Latin version of the ordering of Christ's self-declaration that He is "the way, the truth, and the life" (John 14:6).

Church.[4] This book is Thomistic in that it borrows from the writings and the example of St. Thomas in at least three fundamental ways.

First, a host of good books—ancient, modern, and in between—have been written about the seven deadly sins, but I will aver that no author has addressed the topic in so thorough and complete a manner as did St. Thomas Aquinas. He addressed the deadly sins within his masterwork, the over 3,000-page, 1,500,000-word *Summa Theologica,* in the context of the whole of theology, and in particular, in their relationship to human virtues. Virtues perfect our God-given powers, leading us toward happiness, and ultimately, back toward union with God. To understand how to maximize the virtues that would raise us toward heaven, we must also understand the vices and sins that would hold us down to earth (and possibly, ultimately, even much lower). St. Thomas also addressed these sins in even more depth in his book *De Malo* (*On Evil*), and although our structure will borrow most directly from his *Summa Theologica,* we will also borrow at times from this other great work of the Angelic Doctor.

----

[4] In the course of her two thousand years or so, the Catholic Church has named thirty-five Doctors from among her learned host of saints. In Latin, *docere* means "to teach." These Doctors are the Church's great teachers, and St. Thomas Aquinas, along with St. Augustine, are clearly the most prominent. (Just check out the *Catechism of the Catholic Church,* and you'll see how often they are cited.) St. Thomas is known as both the Angelic Doctor and the Common Doctor—angelic in his demeanor, in his intellect, and in his special attention to angels in his writings and common in that his thought is of universal applicability to all Catholics across the centuries and across the world.

This book is Thomistic in a second important sense: in that St. Thomas sought out *truth* regardless of its origin. Pope Leo XIII wrote in his encyclical *Aeterni Patris*, citing the theologian Cajetan, that St. Thomas seemed to have "inherited the intellect of all" the Church Doctors who came before him, because he so respected them, venerated them, and studied their thoughts until they became as his own. To read the *Summa Theologica* is to become immersed in the thought of scores of ancient Eastern and Western, Greek and Latin Church Fathers and Doctors, seen through the ever clarifying and synthesizing lenses of St. Thomas's penetrating intellect. The same applies to the Scriptures. St. Thomas possessed an astounding knowledge of the Bible, which can be seen most clearly in his biblical commentaries, for example, on the Gospels of Sts. Matthew and John and on the letters of St. Paul. It also rings out from every page of the *Summa Theologica*, including those pages in which he addresses our seven deadly sins.

Even with his mastery of Scripture and the writings of Church Fathers and councils, St. Thomas was not nearly finished in his search for the greatest possible depth and breadth of truth. He also searched out the kernels of truth within the writings of prominent Jewish and Arab theologians, and indeed, he culled thoroughly the writings of ancient pagan philosophers and poets, from Greeks such as Plato and Aristotle, to Romans such as Cicero and Seneca, and from so many more. A man of the deepest faith, St. Thomas also held the deepest respect and gratitude for the natural reason God has implanted in our souls. He would never have thought that the entirety of truth was contained just within his own mountain of writings, and in this regard, we will seek insights on the seven deadly sins from many who came before St. Thomas, as well as those who came after him.

We'll borrow insights here and there on the seven deadly sins (and I'll let you know where with footnotes), from a variety of sources, from ancient and modern psychologists and philosophers, in addition to insights from centuries of great saints. That then is the second sense of our Thomistic approach. We'll seek out the truth about these sins wherever it can be found.

Here's a third and final sense in which our search for truth will be Thomistic. A big problem with a lot of modern theology, philosophy, and psychology is that prominent academic thinkers are prone to write works for each other, for kindred experts within their specialties, employing specialized terminologies and examining ever-finer, theoretical points. Well, although St. Thomas's intellect was extraordinary in its powers, he never let it get lost in the realm of ivory-tower abstractions. Although his mind was angelic and peered into the highest heavens, St. Thomas was always quite down to earth as well. He would write about the contemplative life and about theoretical virtues that seek the truth for its own sake, but he would write about the active life as well and about practical virtues that seek to do good here on earth. His masterful *Summa Theologica* was not written for other master theologians, but for "beginners," as he says in its prologue. St. Thomas always sought truth, but he also sought to share it with others. Indeed, he lived the Dominican motto *Contemplata allis tradere*: to share with others the fruit of one's contemplation.[5]

So then, if this book has achieved its third Thomistic goal, you will walk away at its end not only with an intellectually satisfying grasp of the history, theology, philosophy, and psychology

---

[5] "For even as it is better to enlighten than merely to shine, so it is better to give to others the fruits of one's contemplation than merely to contemplate" (*ST*, II-II, Q. 188, art. 6).

of the seven deadly sins, (not to mention their forty-four "daughters" we'll meet in due course) but also with an arsenal of practical weapons you can use to combat these sins in yourself and in your loved ones, to clear the path for greater virtue, deeper happiness, and more profound union with God.

The Battle Plan

Here, then, is our battle plan, as we lay out the course of this book. In the introductory chapters of part I, we'll explore the history of the concept of the seven deadly sins addressing questions like these:

* Where are the seven deadly sins in the Bible?

* Why are there *seven* of them? (Didn't they start out as *eight*?)

* What did the ancient Eastern, Greek-speaking Church Fathers teach us about these sins?

* How did the ancient Western, Latin-speaking Church Fathers take those ideas and run with them?

* What takes place within our souls when we grapple with these deadly sins?

* Why are these deadly sins sometimes called capital or cardinal sins?

* Why are they sometimes called deadly vices rather than deadly sins?

* Why do some lists differ in different names for the seven deadly sins?

- How can sins have "daughters"?

- How did St. Thomas Aquinas synthesize the great theological literature?

- What kinds of methods have been developed to conquer these deadly sins?

Then, in the heart of our chapters within this book's part II, we'll tackle the deadly sins one by one. In the back half of this book we will come to the "front," so to speak, the front of the field of our spiritual warfare. Here, in our "battle plans" chapters, you'll find a series of specific, practical recommendations for conquering these sins when they rise to wreak havoc in your life, or in the lives of those you love. These will be culled from the writings of St. Thomas, a host of other great saints, and from pagan philosophers and modern psychologists as well. They will focus on psychological strategies of examination for examining your conscience and observing and controlling your emotional reactions, as well as ancient strategies involving the use of Scripture, prayer, and the lessons we can learn from the great saints and from Christ Himself.

Last Things Last

In our concluding chapter, we'll examine the world's deadliest sin, the Queen of the Vices, the capital sin that Pope St. Gregory the Great and St. Thomas Aquinas found even more fundamental and deadly than our "seven deadly sins." We will also examine how this death-dealing sin can be conquered by the Mother of the Virtues. This fountainhead of all virtues can lead us from deadly sin and ultimately to an eternal life of bliss with the Holy Trinity.

The details will have to wait—last things last after all! First things have been first, and now, second things will come second. Let's move from the introduction right into part I. Two thousand years of deadly sins and life-giving saints await us.

The Ancient Family History of the Seven Deadly Sins

"Wretch, tell us the name of your father, the name of the mother who bore you to bring calamity into the world, the names of your loathsome sons and daughters."

And this is how anger replies:

"I come from many sources and I have more than one father. My mothers are Vainglory, Avarice, Greed. And Lust too. My father is named Conceit. My daughters have the names of Remembrance of Wrongs, Hate, Hostility, and Self-Justification."

—ST. JOHN CLIMACUS[6]

[6] John Climacus, *The Ladder of Divine Ascent* (New York: Paulist Press, 1982), 150–151.

CHAPTER 1

Deadly Sins in Sacred Scripture

For all that is in the world, the lust of the flesh,
and the lust of the eyes and the pride of life, is
not of the Father but is of the world. And the
world passes away, and the lust of it; but he
who does the will of God abides forever.

—1 JOHN 2:16–17

So Where in the Bible Are the Seven Deadly Sins?

It is true that the "seven deadly sins" appear nowhere as a neatly numbered list in any book of Sacred Scripture. It is true as well, though, that the ancient family history of the seven deadly sins can be traced all the way back to the earliest origins of man as recounted in the very first book of the Bible. We are told in Genesis how Adam and Eve made choices contrary to the will of God and brought sin into the world and the enduring tendency toward sin into the soul. Further, although what have come to be called the seven deadly sins do not appear together as a list in the Bible, each is in there on its own a truly vast number of times.

On the following page is a simple summary culled from *The Catholic Bible Concordance*.[7] As the charts tallies show, the seven deadly sins are clearly biblical, especially if we bear in mind that the subject matter of these particular sins is also often addressed by description in words of counsel and displayed in the lives and actions of biblical characters, without the sins being explicitly named and adding to our tallies. Indeed, as we

---

[7] C. W. Lyons with Thomas Deliduka, comps., *The Catholic Bible Concordance: Revised Standard Version, Catholic Edition* (Steubenville, OH: Emmaus Road, 2008). Although my math might be off, for the word *sin* I count 528 references, not to mention at least a thousand more if we include variants such as *sinned, sinners, sinning,* and *sins.*

Biblical References to the Seven Deadly Sins

Deadly Sin (and grammatical variants)	Number of Biblical References
Sloth (slothful, slothfulness)	5
Gluttony (glutton, gluttonous, gluttons)	9
Envy (enviable, envied, envious)	13
Lust (lustful, lustfully, lusts, lusty)	23
Greed (greedily, greedy)	27
Pride (proud, proudly)	138
Wrath (wrathful)	274

proceed to examine each of the sins in depth, we will cite and reflect upon scads of those scriptural references and stories (just as St. Thomas did). In fact, let's peruse a small sacred sample of verses in which one or more of what came to be known as the seven deadly sins are discussed:

On *Sloth*
- "Through sloth the roof sinks in, and through indolence the house leaks." (Eccl. 10:18)
- "Slothfulness casts into a deep sleep, and an idle person will suffer hunger." (Prov. 19:15)

On *Gluttony*
- "Be not among winebibbers, or among gluttonous eaters of meat; for the drunkard and the glutton will come to

poverty, and drowsiness will clothe a man with rags."
(Prov. 23:20–21)

- "The distress of sleeplessness and of nausea and colic are with the glutton." (Sir. 31:20)

On Envy

- "But through the devil's envy death entered the world, and those who belong to his party experience it." (Wisd. 2:24)
- "Let us have no self-conceit, no provoking of one another, no envy of one another." (Gal. 5:26)

On Lust

- "The righteousness of the upright delivers them, but the treacherous are taken captive by their lust." (Prov. 11:6)
- "You have heard it said, 'You shall not commit adultery.' But I say to you that every one who looks at a woman lustfully has committed adultery with her in his heart." (Matt. 5:27–28)

On Greed

- "A greedy man's eye is not satisfied with a portion, and mean injustice withers the soul." (Sir. 14:9)
- "His greed is as wide as Sheol; like death he never has enough." (Hab. 2:5)

On Pride

- "For in pride there is ruin and great confusion." (Tob. 4:13)
- "When pride comes, then comes disgrace, but with the humble is wisdom." (Prov. 11:2)

On Wrath

- "A soft answer turns away wrath, but a harsh word stirs up anger." (Prov. 15:1)

- "Let all bitterness and wrath and anger and clamor and slander be put away from you, with all malice, and be kind to one another, tenderhearted, forgiving one another, as God in Christ forgave you." (Eph. 4:31–32)

Now, there are also plenty of places within the books of the Bible in which multiple sins are listed together.

For an example from the Old Testament:

> There are six things which the LORD hates,
> seven which are an abomination to him:
> haughty eyes, a lying tongue,
> and hands that shed innocent blood,
> a heart that devised wicked plans,
> feet that make haste to run to evil,
> a false witness who breathes out lies,
> and a man who sows discord among brothers.
> (Prov. 6:16–19)

And for a couple examples from the New Testament:

For from within, out of the heart of man, come evil thoughts, fornication, theft, murder, adultery, coveting, wickedness, deceit, licentiousness, envy, slander, pride, foolishness. All of these evil things come from within, and they defile a man. (Mark 7:21–23)

Now the works of the flesh are plain: immorality, impurity, licentiousness, idolatry, sorcery, enmity, strife, jealousy, anger, selfishness, dissension, party spirit, envy, drunken-ness, carousing, and the like. (Gal. 5:19–21)

Our example from Proverbs lists *seven* abominations, although they do not exactly match what have come to be known as the seven deadly sins. Mark's Gospel lists *thirteen* evil things that come from within the heart of man, several of which would find their way to the list of seven deadly sins. St. Paul's list, although incomplete (ending in "and the like"), includes a full *fifteen* "works of the flesh."[8] The quotation from St. John that headed this chapter referred to *three classes* of sins: the lust of the flesh, the lust of the eyes, and the pride of life. So how then did we arrive at what have been known for over fourteen hundred years as the *seven* deadly sins? Well, I thought you'd never ask. Indeed, that's what the first part of this book is all about. Prepare yourself for the intriguing family history of the seven deadly sins.

---

[8] Which he promptly proceeded to contrast with countervailing fruits of the Holy Spirit: "love, joy, peace, patience, kindness, goodness, faithfulness, gentleness, self-control" (Gal. 5:22–23).

CHAPTER 2

Evagrius Ponticus's Eight Assailing Thoughts

> The Spirit immediately drove him out into the wilderness. And he was in the wilderness forty days, tempted by Satan; and he was with the wild beasts; and the angels ministered to him.
>
> —MARK 1:12–13

> The most generic thoughts, in which every thought is included, are eight in all. First, the thought of gluttony, and after it that of fornication, third that of avarice, fourth that of distress, fifth that of anger, sixth that of listless depression (*akedia*), seventh that of vanity, eighth that of pride. It is not up to us whether any of these disturb the soul or not. But it is up to us whether they linger (*khronizein*) or not, or whether they stir up emotions or not.
>
> —EVAGRIUS PONTICUS, *PRACTICAL TREATISE*, 6[9]

---

[9] Cited in Richard Sorabji, *Emotion and Peace of Mind: From Stoic Agitation to Christian Temptation* (New York, Oxford University Press, 2000), 359.

A Desert Full of Temptations

The origins of our modern list of seven deadly sins are usually traced back to one Evagrius of Pontus (A.D. 345–399). Although he did *not* really refer to them as *sins*, and his list was not seven but eight items long, his primacy of place in this genealogy is indeed well warranted.

Evagrius was a man of broad philosophical knowledge and of deep Christian faith. Ordained as a lector in 380 by St. Basil the Great in Neocaesarea (modern-day Turkey) and as a deacon in 382 by St. Gregory Nazianus in Constantinople, Evagrius is best known for his life and his writings while living as a monk in semi-isolation in the sandy deserts of Egypt.

Ancient biographies relate that earlier in life he was consumed with vanity due to the praise and acclaim he achieved for his powers as a preacher. He was also so beleaguered by an infatuation with a married woman that he eventually fled Constantinople to a monastery near Jerusalem. There he received spiritual guidance from Melania the Elder, a Sister who had founded a religious community of women on the Mount of Olives. In 385 Evargius would join a monastic community at Nitria in Lower Egypt, and finally, in his last years of life, he lived at another nearby monastic community deep in the heart of the Egyptian desert. Evagrius expounded some views about God that showed

the influence of the theologian Origen and that were later considered heretical, but his value to us comes from the way he wrote
about those eight precursors — the ancestors, we might say — of
the seven deadly sins.

Modern life in the crowded city is certainly full of temptations, as I'm sure most readers would agree. Even sixteen hundred
years ago, Evagrius found the case the same. He fled city life but
found, as did his Savior before him, that even the depths of the
desert provide no relief from evil temptations. Evagrius lived at
times in *cenobitic* (monastic) communities in which monks spent
most of their time in their own small individual huts and met
on occasion for communal activities. Much of their time was
spent in solitary work and prayer, and yet, being fallen human
beings, despite their aims of holiness, their minds were still often
assaulted by temptations toward various kinds of sin. In his *Practical Treatises*, Evagrius wrote about eight evil *logismoi* (thoughts)
that would assail him and his fellow desert monks. Here they are:

Evagrius's List of Eight Evil Thoughts

1. Gluttony (*gastrimargia*)
2. Fornication (*porneia*)
3. Avarice (*philarguria*)
4. Distress (*lupe* or *lypi*)
5. Anger (*orge*)
6. Depression (*akedia*)
7. Vanity (*kenodoxia*)
8. Pride (*hyperephania*)

For Evagrius, these were generic or general thoughts that tempt
us toward a variety of sins. He saw them as natural stirrings, what
the Stoic philosophers such as the Roman Seneca called "first

movements"—that is, nearly automatic or reflexive thoughts that arise within us and disturb our souls in a fleeting, pre-emotional sense. It is up to us whether we will choose to dwell on them, leading to harmful, sinful emotions and actions. Per Evagrius, "It is not up to us whether any of these disturb the soul or not. But it is up to us whether they linger (*khronizein*) or not, or whether they stir up emotions or not."[10]

Evagrius noted that these evil thoughts can be stirred within us by demons, but they can also arise from within our own souls. He analyzed some of these evil thoughts in depth, for example, *akedia* (or acedia), the "noonday demon,"[11] which centuries later would come to be known as *sloth*. He provided remedies as well, employing asceticism and prayer, pitting virtuous thoughts and scriptural verses against them, and even, for spiritual beginners, pitting one evil thought against the other. We'll examine some of his suggestions when we address the remedies to the deadly sins in our complete chapters on each of them. For now we must move on to see how the eight evil thoughts headed west from the deserts of Egypt all the way to the south coast of France.

---

[10] Sorabji, *Emotion and Peace of Mind*, 359.
[11] This derives from Psalm 91:6: "The destruction that wastes at noonday" (RSV). We'll address this noonday demon in the full light of day when we come to chapter 8 on the nature of sloth and the ways to defeat it.

CHAPTER 3

St. John Cassian's Eight Deadly Vices

And Jesus, full of the Holy Spirit, returned from
the Jordan, and was led by the Spirit for forty
days in the wilderness, tempted by the devil.

—LUKE 4:1–2

There are eight principal vices that attack humankind. The first is gluttony, which means the vora-
ciousness of the belly; the second is fornication;
the third is filargyria, which is avarice or love of
money; the fourth is anger; the fifth is sadness;
the sixth acedia, which is anxiety or weariness of
heart; the seventh is cenodoxia, which is boast-
fulness or vainglory; and the eighth is pride.

—ST. JOHN CASSIAN[12]

---

[12] All citations of Cassian are from St. John Cassian,
The Conferences (New York: Newman Press, 1997),
183–196, as cited at http://pigizois.net/agglika/on_
the_eight_deadly_sins.htm, retrieved on June 7,
2014.

Deadly Sins Go West

Evagrius's list of eight evil thoughts headed west when it was transplanted and espoused by St. John Cassian (A.D. 360–435). Cassian was born in Scythia Minor (modern-day Romania) and lived for a time in a monastery in Bethlehem and later with the Desert Fathers in Egypt. He was ordained a deacon in 399 by St. John Chrysostom at Constantinople, and then, in 403, upon Chrysostom's exile, headed west to what is now Marseilles, France. He became a priest there and founded a monastery for men and one for women. His most famous writings are his *Institutes* and *Conferences*.

In the *Conferences*, Cassian reports that he learned of "eight principal vices that attack humankind" from a very old monk named Serapion. The evil eight (gluttony, fornication, avarice, anger, sadness, acedia, vainglory, and pride), you will note, are essentially the same as those of our other Egyptian desert monk, Evagrius. He also provides some very interesting and useful analysis of the psychological nature of these sins, as well as their theological nature and their impact on the state of our souls as spelled out for us in Scripture.

For example, he classifies two kinds of vices, "natural" vices such as gluttony and unnatural vices such as avarice. He reports "four kinds of operations" as well:

Operations	Vices
Cannot be completed without bodily actions	Gluttony Fornication
Can be completed without bodily actions	Pride Vainglory
Motivated by external causes	Avarice Anger
Motivated by internal causes	Acedia Sadness

Gluttony and fornication "are in us naturally" and are "carnal" in that they arise from natural stirrings of the flesh,[13] yet they require external matter (food, drink, bodies) to be fully consummated. As Cassian supports with Scripture, "But every man is tempted, when he is drawn away of his own lust, and enticed. The lust hath conceived, it bringeth forth sin; and sin, when it is finished, bringeth forth death" (James 1:14–15). Here we see the sequence of a carnal sin in action, and we see how it can become "deadly." "Spiritual" sins, on the contrary (the remaining six vices), don't provide fleshly pleasure and may even result in great suffering.

Cassian notes as well that while the eight vices have "different origins and varying operations," six of them bear a special interconnection, acting in essence, we might say today, just like six deadly dominoes. Each of these sins overflows into the next one. Gluttony, said Cassian, like many other ancient and

[13] Deriving form the Latin *caro, carnis* for meat or flesh.

medieval Church Fathers, can lead to fornication. From there, wrote Cassian, fornication leads to avarice, avarice to anger, anger to sadness, and sadness to that spiritual listlessness of acedia. The last two vices, vainglory and pride, were seen to be linked in a similar way, so that an excess of vanity opens the door to pride. These interconnections, in turn, led to the interesting recommendation to attack any sin that hounds us by attacking those that precede it in the chain.

Eight Deadly Dominoes
Gluttony > Fornication > Avarice > Anger > Sadness > Acedia
Vainglory > Pride

Cassian also noted that the eight deadly vices can be divided into four related couples that are especially prone to promote each other: gluttony and fornication, avarice and anger, sadness and acedia, and again, vainglory and pride.

Four Deadly Couples

Gluttony and Fornication	Avarice and Anger
Sadness and Acedia	Vainglory and Pride

Cassian also distinguished different ways in which each deadly vice can be manifested;[14] for example, three kinds of gluttony (eating too soon, too much, or in too picky a manner), three kinds of fornication (in the union of the sexes, alone, and in thought), three kinds of avarice (reluctance to be deprived of wealth and property, covetousness to have returned what was distributed to

---

[14] But for pride, which he did not include in this particular analysis in his *Conferences*. St. Thomas refers to these as "species" of sins.

the poor, and desire for more than what one possessed before), three kinds of anger ("blazing up" interiorly, acting out in word and deed, and holding a grudge), two kinds of sadness (sadness that comes after anger ceases after one is thwarted and another born of unreasonable mental anguish or despair), two kinds of acedia (one that prompts excessive sleep and one that encourages a person to flee from his home), two kinds of vainglory (being

Eighteen Varieties of Cassian's Deadly Vices

Deadly Vices	Specific Kinds
Gluttony	Eating too soon Eating too much Eating in too picky a manner
Fornication	In the union of the sexes Alone In thought
Avarice	Reluctance to be deprived Covetousness for return of what was given Desire for more than possessed before
Anger	Blazing up inside Acting out in word and deed Bearing a grudge over time
Sadness	After anger ceases when one is thwarted Unreasonable anguish or despair
Acedia	One that prompts excessive sleep One that encourages one to flee from home
Vainglory	Being uplifted by external, carnal things Being inflamed by praise for spiritual, hidden things

uplifted because of carnal and external things and being inflamed by others' praise "because of spiritual and hidden things").

In his last section on these vices, Cassian discussed various ways to fight them. He noted that while these vices "disturb the whole human race," each of us may be more or less afflicted by any one or more of these vices. Indeed, we see even in our day how a person who seems firmly and obviously in the clutches of one particular vice may become known as a glutton, a lecher, a miser, a hothead, a sourpuss, a slacker, a prima donna, a narcissist, and the like. From these individual differences in susceptibility to sin may come the need for different battle plans and different weapons for each person. *In general, Cassian recommends expending the most effort in conquering the vices that have most conquered us.* We'll discuss his particular methods later, but let us note for now his chief caution—should we begin to win the spiritual struggle against sin:

> Namely, when you have enjoyed a notable success in warring against the carnal vices and you see that you have been freed from their filthiness and from this world's way of life, you should not be puffed up with the success of the struggle and the victory and ascribe this to your own strength and wisdom, believing that you were able to obtain victory over evil spirits and carnal vices through your own efforts and application and free will. There is no doubt that you would never have been able to prevail over these if the Lord's help had not fortified and protected you.

CHAPTER 4

Prudentius's Bloody Battle of Vices versus Virtues

When Abram heard that his kinsman had been
taken captive, he led forth his trained men ... and
went in pursuit.... And he divided his forces against
them by night ... and routed them and pursued
them to Hobah.... Then he brought back all the
goods, and also brought back his kinsman Lot
with his goods, and the women and the people.

— GENESIS 14:14–16

Thou, O Christ, art God born of the Father — say, our
King, with what fighting force the soul is furnished
and enabled to expel the sins from within our breast;
when there is disorder among our thoughts and
rebellion arises within us, when the strife of our
evil passions vexes the spirit, say what help here is
then to guard her liberty, what array with superior
force withstands the fiendish raging in our heart.

— PRUDENTIUS'S *PSYCHOMACHIA*[15]

[15] H. J. Thomson, trans., *Prudentius*, vol. 1 (Cambridge,
MA: Harvard University Press, 2006), 279.

Are You Ready to Rumble? The Battle for the Human Soul

Aurelius Prudentius Clemens (A.D. 348–413) was most likely born in what was then known as Caesaraugusta and today as Sarragosa (or Zaragoza) in the Aragon region of northeast Spain. If you haven't heard of him, perhaps that is because he was never declared a saint or a Church Father or Doctor. Neither was he a monk, a priest, or a trained theologian. Prudentius, rather, was an administrative official of the later Roman Empire and an early Christian literary figure.

A man of deep respect for Roman literature and of deep Catholic faith, he strove to carry on and Christianize the style and literary forms of the great classical Latin poets, such as Virgil and Horace, both in lyrical odes and in moving epics. His hymns—for example, "For a Cock-Crow," "A Morning Hymn," "A Hymn before Meat," "A Hymn for the Lighting of the Lamp," "A Hymn before Sleep," indeed, even "A Hymn for Every Hour"—show a deep knowledge of Scripture, a pious devotion to Christ and His Catholic Church, a vivid imagination, and in this literary amateur's opinion, although a bit on the flowery and melodramatic side, they are very much worth reading today, even in translation. In his "Hymn before Sleep," for example, after invoking and describing the Holy Trinity, we find these lines:

But while kindly repose spreads all through our body, and so sleep floods it, lulls the heart to rest from labour, the spirit roams free through the air, quick and lively, and in diverse figures sees things that are hidden; for the mind, whose source is heaven and whose pure font is from the skies, cannot lie idle when left from care.[16]

It seems that Prudentius's own creative mind was not one to lie idle while sleeping or while awake, and this is especially apparent in the work for which he enters our history of the seven deadly sins. Prudentius penned the *Psychomachia*,[17] translated in the Loeb Classical Library edition as *The Fight for Mansoul*, in a very dramatic, graphic, almost dreamlike manner. Embracing the ancient Roman penchant for personifying abstract ideas,[18] Prudentius would present, in about thirty-five pages, a rip-roaring battle between worldly vices and Christian virtues. The theme of using virtue to conquer vice is a very old one, and one we'll examine in depth in every one of our chapter's "battle plans" sections, but rarely has it been presented so graphically.

---

[16] Thomson, *Prudentius*, vol. 1, 51.

[17] From the Greek words *psukhē* for "spirit" and *makhē* for "battle," although the poem itself was written in Latin.

[18] St. Thomas Aquinas himself, nine centuries later, would recommend rendering abstract ideas into something concrete we can mentally picture. "Now the reason for the necessity of finding these illustrations or images is that simple and spiritual impressions easily slip from the mind, unless they be tied to some corporal image, because human knowledge has a great hold on sensible objects" (*ST*, II-II, Q. 49, art. 1). (It seems mostly likely, though, that Prudentius was more interested in the images' dramatic literary effect than the fact that they help us remember.)

The *Psychomachia* is rife with scriptural allusions, theological reflections, and classical mythological allusions. A description of Abraham's battle to win back his nephew Lot from his captivity by Mesopotamian kings[19] sets the stage, and within just a few pages, we are in the midst of a spiritual battlefield as graphic and gory as the blood-soaked plains outside the walls of the Troy of Homer's *Iliad*. Behold a relatively tame episode of the battle:

> Lo, first Worship-of-the-Old Gods ventures to match her strength against Faith's challenge and strike at her. But she, rising higher, smites her foe's head down, with its fillet-decked brows, lays in the dust that mouth that was sated with the blood of beasts, and tramples the eyes under foot, squeezing them out in death.[20]

Although the details of the blows of battle and the resulting bloody carnage echo Homer, Prudentius provides decidedly Judeo-Christian twists. Pride, for example, after "galloping about, all puffed up,"[21] and mercilessly haranguing the virtue of Lowliness as an enemy beneath her contempt, proceeds to be thrown from her horse when she charges into a concealed pit, laid out for the enemy by her ally Deceit. Prudentius was well aware that "pride goes before destruction, and a haughty spirit before a fall" (Prov. 16:18). Pride is then conquered by Lowliness, along with her ally Hope.

A host of Christian virtues are arrayed on the field in one-on-one battle with an opposing host of pagan vices. Dozens of

---

[19] Gen. 14.
[20] Prudentius, *Psychomachia*, 281.
[21] Ibid., 293.

vices and virtues team up with one another to play supportive roles, but these are the seven key matchups:

Prudentius's Bloody Battle of Vices versus Virtues

In this corner . . .	*And in this corner . . .*
7 Deadly Vices	*7 Heavenly Virtues*
Idolatry (worship of the old gods)	Faith
Lust	Chastity
Wrath	Patience (or longanimity)
Pride	Lowliness (and hope)
Indulgence	Sobriety
Greed	Charitable works
Discord (heresy)	Concord (and faith)

Lust, wrath, pride, indulgence, and greed should seem rather familiar, since they can pretty easily be matched with the thoughts or vices of fornication, anger, pride, gluttony, and avarice in the lists of Evagrius and Cassian. Missing here are acedia, distress, and vainglory, and in their place we find idolatry and discord. Why the differences?

Well, Prudentius was not a desert monk of the East, but a citified lay poet of the West. His background and his audience certainly differed from the monks', and perhaps this is why vices such as idolatry and discord appear as central figures in Prudentius's battle and not on the lists of Evagrius and Cassian. Prudentius was speaking to a pagan as well as a Christian audience. Idolatry personified those who clung to the old gods of Rome, while he specifically identified discord with heresy. Indeed, in

PRUDENTIUS'S BATTLE OF VICES VERSUS VIRTUES

translation we read, "I am called Discord, and my other name is Heresy."[22] Discord appears *after* the Christian virtues have apparently defeated the pagan vices and Peace has arrived on the scene. Surely Prudentius was well aware that Christ Himself had many times prayed that His Church would be as one,[23] yet even in His time, many a heresy had already sprouted among Christians. In the end, Faith and Concord do triumph over Discord since the two are "sisters sworn in holy alliance in the love of Christ."[24]

Prudentius then provides a dramatic little side branch in our family history of the seven deadly sins. His *Battle for Man's Soul* is unique and entertaining reading (for those who like that kind of thing), and it is not without theological and spiritual interest and merit. For now, though, we must return to the main trunk of the history of the seven deadly sins, a trunk that sprouted forth above the hot, dry sands of the Eastern monastic tradition.

[22] "Discordia dicor, cognomento Heresis" (ibid., 329).
[23] Cf. John 17:11–23.
[24] Prudentius, *Psychomachia*, 331, v. 736.

CHAPTER 5

Climacus's Divine Ascent Away from Sinful Passions

Jacob left Beersheba, and went toward Haran. And
he came to a certain place, and stayed there that
night, because the sun had set. Taking one of the
stones of the place, he put it under his head and
lay down in that place to sleep. And he dreamed
that there was a ladder set up on the earth, and the
top of it reached to heaven; and behold, the angels
of God were ascending and descending on it!

— GENESIS 28:10–12

Ascend, my brothers, ascend eagerly. Let your
hearts' resolve be to climb. Listen to the voice
of the one who says: "Come, let us go up to the
mountain of the Lord, to the house of our God"
(Isa. 2:3), Who make our feet to be like the feet of
the deer, "Who sets us on the high places, that
we may be triumphant on His road" (Hab. 3:19).

— ST. JOHN CLIMACUS,
THE LADDER OF DIVINE ASCENT

Climbing Jacob's Ladder

We return now to the deserts of the East to meet St. John Climacus (A.D. 525–606). This great Church Father, esteemed in the East and the West, became a novice at a monastery at age sixteen, spent twenty years in isolation studying the lives of the saints, and died at a monastery at Mount Sinai, having been elected abbot at the age of seventy. One of the quotations that starts our chapter is from an exhortation in his most notable book, the superb and enduring spiritual classic *The Ladder of Divine Ascent*. Here the reader is guided through thirty chapters called steps, each devoted to building higher levels of physical and spiritual ascetic virtues. Among the highest of special value to monks are prayer, stillness, and dispassion. The highest step of the ladder (echoing St. Paul's appraisal of the virtues in 1 Corinthians 13:13) is *agape*, or love.

The metaphorical ladder borrows from Jacob's ladder. Genesis 28:10–16 relates how Jacob dreamed of a ladder on which angels ascended into heaven and descended to earth. Climacus's ladder is a ladder of "divine ascent," or spiritual perfection, and he concludes his book by telling us why the ladder has thirty steps and why the highest of them is love:

> Baptized at the thirtieth year of His earthly age, Christ attained the thirtieth step on the spiritual ladder, or God

49

indeed is love, and to Him be praise, dominion, power. In Him is the cause, past, present, and future, of all this is good forever and ever. Amen.[25]

Here then we see another recurring theme in the early treatments of the seven deadly sins. It is Christ who ultimately conquered sin and only through Him that we can do so as well. Later, we will see how St. Thomas would describe stages of spiritual perfection that start with the battle against sins, continue with the struggle to build virtues, and culminate, at the end, in union with God, all made possible and aided by God's gratuitous grace. Climacus's ladder makes such progression very clear indeed, guiding us through it, indeed, step by step!

Although Climacus wrote specifically for the desert monks of his day, his book is rich in lessons for all of us, regardless of locale, vocation, or time. After relating seven steps specific to monastic life (renunciation, detachment, and exile) and four concomitant foundational virtues (obedience, penitence, remembrance of death, and sorrow), Climacus spends steps 8 through 23 addressing how to conquer a series of sinful passions (anger, malice, slander, talkativeness, falsehood, despondency, gluttony, lust, avarice, insensitivity, fear, vainglory, pride, and blasphemy). Although that list includes fourteen sinful passions, he also writes about seven as more fundamental than other sins. He was well aware of Evagrius's eight assailing thoughts and was certainly influenced by him (although in one place, he derides Evagrius's prescription for taming gluttony by eating only bread and water as being unrealistic and ineffective).

---

[25] St. John Climacus, *The Ladder of Divine Ascent.*

When describing several fundamental sinful passions in step 29, Climacus lists *seven* and notes a precedent for this number in the writings of "Gregory Theologos." Climacus's contemporary St. Gregory Nazianus (330–390), one of the four original Doctors of the Eastern Church, is indeed known in the East as Gregory the Theologian, and yet there is no known list of seven such sins in his extant writings. On the other hand, or on the other side of the world, so to speak, there was another contemporary known in the West as Gregory Dialogus, because of the famous *Dialogues* he wrote. In a modern introduction to Climacus's *Ladder of Divine Ascent*, Kallistos Ware speculates "perhaps 'Theologos' is a scribal error for 'Dialogus.'"[26] This other Gregory is another story, indeed, one that we'll address in the very next chapter.

For now, let's take a look at St. John Climacus's list:

St. John Climacus's Seven Sinful Passions
1. Gluttony
2. Lechery (lust)
3. Cupidity (avarice or greed)
4. Despondency
5. Anger
6. Vainglory
7. Pride

Here, we pretty much see seven of the eight sins that were found in Evagrius and in St. John Cassian. Which sin is missing? Distress (*lupe* or *lypi*) is not found here, because Climacus, like the Western Gregory, considered it essentially the same sin as despondency (or *akedia*). As we'll see in the next chapter, this

---

[26] Ibid., 64.

is still not exactly the same seven that would come down to us primarily through Pope St. Gregory, but again, hold that thought until our next chapter. For now, there's much more to glean from the steps of Jacob's (and Climacus's) ladder.

We got a glimpse of how St. John Cassian noted special relationships and linkages between deadly sins. Recall his chains of six and of two that we referred to as "deadly dominoes" in chapter 3. Recall as well his four deadly couplets. For Climacus, heavenly virtues form the steps of our ladder toward heaven, but deadly sins form an interlinking chain that would hold us down to earth. Ware has culled out the links from Climacus's steps 8 through 23,[27] which I'll present here like steps leading down from a ladder, each sin leading to the one below it:

Anger
Malice
Slander
Talkativeness
Falsehood
Despondency
Lust
Insensitivity ("unbelief")
Vainglory
Fear
Pride
Blasphemy

As the divine ladder leads to the gates of heaven, this one, we might say, can descend to the gates at the very bowels of hell. It's certainly one ladder we'll hope to sidestep, and Climacus

[27] St. John Climacus, *The Ladder of Divine Ascent*, 65.

gives plenty of advice on how to avoid it. We'll borrow aplenty from this sage's specific advice in the chapters of this book's part II. For now, though, we'll take a glance at his thoughtful analysis of the general nature of these sins, and how they may grow and fester in the human mind and give birth to sinful thoughts, words, and deeds.

In his chapter on the fifteenth step, that of chastity, Climacus borrows from the writings of other early Desert Fathers[28] and lays out a sixfold sequence through which sinful passions may be either chastised or inflamed, and here are the six stages:

St. John Climacus's Stages
of the Growth of Sinful Passions

1. Provocation
2. Coupling
3. Assent
4. Captivity
5. Struggle
6. Passion

1. *Provocation* is described as a simple word or image that we experience for the first time and, in the instant that it affects us, is said to enter into our heart. Climacus notes that this first stage is not sinful.

2. *Coupling* is that conversation we have within ourselves regarding that word or image of provocation,

---

[28] Ibid., 182. The modern translator of *The Ladder of Divine Ascent* provides examples of St. Mark the Asectic's *On the Spiritual Laws* and St. Maximos the Confessor's *On Love* in a footnote.

with or without passion. This stage may be sinful, depending on what we have to say to ourselves and the way we say it.

3. *Assent* can be best expressed in the words (translated) of Climacus himself: "the delighted yielding of the soul to what it has encountered.... The condition of the soul determines whether or not the third is sinful."[29]

4. *Captivity* is "a forcible and unwilling abduction of the heart, a permanent lingering with what we have encountered and which totally undermines the necessary order of our souls." Captivity is judged for its sinfulness in terms of the situation, such as whether it occurs at prayer or at other times, and its subject matter, such as whether it is in regards to something trivial or "in the context of evil thoughts."

5. *Struggle* implies the internal struggle against the building attack against the soul and whether one marshals sufficient power of the soul to counter the attack or succumbs to the pleasures of desire.

6. *Passion* is the result of a lost struggle that may remain hidden within the soul but acts to become like a habit,[30] until the soul clings to it of its own will "with affection."

---

[29] St. John Climacus, *The Ladder of Divine Ascent*, 182 (as are all quotations for these stages).

[30] We will see in part II that Thomas lays great emphasis on the power of vices or habits to lead us into sinful behaviors and calls the seven deadly sins "seven capital vices," vices being literally vicious habits.

Passion, says Climacus, is always denounced as sin and calls for either repentance or future punishment.

That sequence rings some bells with me. Do you hear any ringing? Climacus has provided an insightful analysis of psychological and moral processes as common in twenty-first-century America as they were in the fourth century in the deserts of the East. And let's highlight one last contribution of Climacus to the "family history" of the seven deadly sins. We'll read all about these sins' "daughters" in the chapters ahead on Pope St. Gregory and St. Thomas Aquinas. I'll simple note here that Climacus provides quite a dramatic genealogy of the deadly sins.

Review, if you will, our quotation that starts our own part I. Here, the sin of Anger or Wrath is called to account "before the tribunal of reason" and asked to reveal his father, his mother, his sons, and his daughters. Anger does this with an intriguing account of his forebears and heirs.[31] Climacus held such a tribunal for many deadly sins, and they also were forced to admit the enemies who can imprison them. Anger admitted that his foes included Lowliness, and that it was Humility that laid a trap for him. We'll look at those foes again in part II of this book, as we lay up our own plans to defeat the seven deadly sins and all their deadly clans as well.

Next, let's turn to the Church Father who some might well say is also the Father of the List of the Seven Deadly Sins.

---

[31] In case you are not inclined to flip back, Anger reported that it had more than one father, and one that he named was Deceit, and that its mothers are Vainglory, Avarice, Greed, and Lust, and its daughters are Remembrance of Wrongs, Hate, Hostility, and Self-Justification.

CHAPTER 6

Pope St. Gregory the Great and the Seven Deadly Sins

When the trumpet sounds, he says, "Aha!"
He smells the battle from afar, the thunder of the captains, and the shouting.

— JOB 39:25

For the tempting vices, which fight against us in
invisible contest in behalf of the pride which reigns
over them, some of them go first, like captains,
others follow, after the manner of an army.
For all faults do not occupy the heart with equal
access. But while the greater and the few surprise
a neglected mind, the smaller and the number-
less pour themselves upon it in a whole body.

— POPE ST. GREGORY THE GREAT,
THE BOOK OF MORALS[32]

---

[32] *The Book of the Morals of Pope Gregory the Great* or
An Exposition of the Book of Blessed Job, vol. 3, part
6, ch. 31, par. 85, http://www.lectionarycentral.com/
GregoryMoralia/Book31.html.

And Then There Were Seven

Pope St. Gregory the Great (A.D. 540–604) is perhaps the least known of the four original Latin Doctors of the Church — Sts. Ambrose, Augustine, and Jerome being the three others. He is perhaps best known as the namesake of the ancient, beautiful, and reverent form of praise known as Gregorian chant, but we need to know him as well as the Father of the Seven Deadly Sins — the *list* of those sins, that is, for Gregory himself has told us *who* the father of the actual seven sins themselves is, and that we soon will see.

Gregory was born at a time when the classical Latin world was all but shattered. Rome had long been conquered by the Ostrogoths, and the Lombards were poised to dominate the Italian peninsula by Gregory's late twenties. It was a time when many, including Gregory, believed the end of the world was at hand, a time some historians have called the dawn of the Dark Ages.

The son of a Roman senator, Gregory was born into power and wealth. In the year 573, while in his early thirties, Gregory held the office of prefect of Rome, in charge of the great city's administration. Like Prudentius, he held office in the imperial Roman state. Not long after, though, he experienced a deep conversion of heart, and like Evagrius, Cassian, and Climacus before him, he became a monk. He gave his property up for religious uses and turned his palace into a monastery.

Gregory, although known as a man of action, was by nature a man of deep contemplation, and this he sought in his monastic station. Perhaps this is where his contemplation on the nature of the deadly sins began. It would be expressed in his great *Moralia*, a massive commentary on the book of Job.

The world continued to seek Gregory out, however, and Pope Pelagius II made him apostolic legate to the court of the Byzantine emperor at Constantinople.[33] By the year 590, this sought-after monk would be elected pope, an office he would hold and exercise so adeptly during the last fourteen years of his life that he would become one of the few to be known as "the Great."

So what has Great Gregory to do with the seven deadly sins? Now it's time to get down to business. We've seen that Gregory's monastic forebears, Evagrius and St. John Cassian in particular, made famous their lists of *eight* deadly thoughts or principal vices.[34] It may seem a bit of a paradox, that in one sense, Gregory did indeed keep to *eight*, yet he is known for his list of *seven* capital

---

[33] Formerly known as Byzantium, currently as Istanbul, and then the capital of the still surviving eastern half of the Roman Empire, established in 324 by the Christian Roman emperor Constantine the Great.

[34] Prudentius did include seven personified sins as the primary villains in his war for man's soul, but, as we saw, his selection of sins diverged from his predecessors, he did not provide deep theological reflections, and his work was not as influential as that of Evagrius and Cassian. Climacus wrote of eight in some places and seven in others. His work was not as influential as Gregory's was in the Latin West, and he wrote his *Ladder of Divine Ascent* about the year 600, about half a decade after the completion of Gregory's *Moralia*.

sins. Let's do a side-by-side comparison with Evagrius and see how this came about:

Evagrius's and Gregory's Lists

Evagrius's Eight Assailing Thoughts	Gregory's Seven Capital Sins
Gluttony (*gastrimargia*)	Gluttony (*gulia*)
Fornication (*porneia*)	Lust (*luxuria*)
Avarice (*philarguria*)	Avarice (*avaritia*)
Distress (*lupe* or *lypi*)	**Envy** (*invidia*)
Anger (*orge*)	Anger (*ira*)
Depression (*akedia*)	Melancholy (*tristia*)
Vanity (*kenodoxia*)	Vainglory (*vana gloria*)
Pride (*hyperephania*)	

The similarities are most apparent, probably largely because of the influence of St. John Cassian in the West in general, and on Gregory, in particular. Cassian's list, as we saw, was essentially that of Evagrius. The boldface words in our chart highlight the differences. Gregory has removed *distress* or *lupe* from the list, seeing it is essentially the same as *acedia* (*tristia* in Latin), so he is then down to seven. He has, however, added a most important sin absent from earlier lists, that of *envy* (*invidia*), a sorry sin in which we are saddened by another person's good. Well, that makes eight. Gregory then removed *pride* from his list. Did he think that pride was not a deadly sin? No, not at all; in fact, he saw it as the deadliest of all, as the most fundamental of all sins, giving rise to even these seven. Indeed, Gregory cites Scripture here to make his intentions clear:

Pride is the beginning of all sin (Ecclus. 10:15). But seven principal vices, as its first progeny, spring doubtless from this poisonous root, namely, vainglory, envy, anger, melancholy, avarice, gluttony, lust. For, because He grieved that we were held captive by these seven sins of pride, therefore, our Redeemer came to the spiritual battle of our liberation, full of the spirit of sevenfold grace. (*Moralia*, 31.87)

Smelling Sins from Afar

The most common metaphors for the nature of sin and of our attempts to avoid it are those of medicine and of warfare. This will be made clearest in part II, where we will examine the various remedies, and battle plans, that sundry saints and theologians have proposed to heal or to conquer the seven deadly sins. For now, in his *Moralia* explicating the book of Job, we find Gregory clearly in the warfare camp.

Another common feature of all our ancient writers on the deadly sins has been their scriptural context. The Desert Fathers, such as Evagrius, Cassian, and Climacus, all modeled their retreats to the desert to battle temptation toward sin first and foremost on Jesus Christ Himself, who, as the Gospels tell us, went out to the desert to pray and was tempted by the devil. Prudentius's literary battle of vices and virtues drew inspiration from Homer's *Iliad* and Virgil's *Aeneid*, but he begins the warfare with a description of Abraham's battle described in the book of Genesis. Climacus's primary inspiration for his *Ladder of Divine Ascent*, as we saw, was the description of Jacob's dream of a ladder to heaven, also found in Genesis. Gregory too has an explicit scriptural starting point, from which he jumps into the fray of the deadly sins. This we saw in the quotation that started this chapter: "When the trumpet sounds, he says, 'Aha!' He smells the battle from afar, the thunder of the captains, and the shouting" (Job 39:25).

The "captains," Gregory tells us, are the seven deadly sins. Their commander in chief is the sin of pride, and those captains lead an army that follows them. The seven deadly sins are often referred to as *capital* sins. This derives from the Latin word *caput*, meaning "head." (Think about it. Where do you wear your baseball *cap?*)

Of course, when we speak of capital sins, we are using *head* in the sense of the person in charge, who directs other people; the person who forms the goals, issues the commands, and gets the ball rolling. Gregory portrayed the seven deadly sins as captains, and at times as generals, leading a vast and deadly army. The soldiers are a multitudinous variety of sins and misdeeds, and the capital sins are the officers who set them to their nefarious tasks. Pope St. Gregory builds all this dramatic moral exegesis on that verse of a mighty horse that smells a battle coming and hears the thunder and shouting of approaching evil captains with their deadly hordes.

St. Gregory's treatment of the deadly sins would be carried on and expanded in the writings of St. Thomas Aquinas, so we'll come across it again and again. For now, we will highlight just a few key contributions of this government official turned monk turned pope.

First, we saw that Gregory removed *distress* from his list of seven, feeling it was already addressed with *acedia*, or what would become known as *sloth*. Next, he was wise to add a very important and deadly sin, that of the *envy* of another's good. Also, he gave *pride* special pride of place, removing it from the list of seven by counting it as the father of all seven.

Pope St. Gregory the Great's

Vainglory	Envy	Anger	Melancholy
Disobedience	Hatred	Strife	Malice
Boastfulness	Whispering	Swelling of the mind	Rancor
Hypocrisy	Detraction	Insults	Cowardice
Contention	Joy at another's misfortune	Clamor	Despair
Obstinacy	Grief at another's prosperity	Indignation	Slothfulness in fulfilling commands
Discord		Blasphemies	Wandering of the mind on unlawful things
Presumption of novelties			

Seven Sins in Their Chain of Command

Gregory, like Cassian, divides and groups the capital sins according to their similarities and differences. Gregory notes that five of these sins are *spiritual* (vainglory, envy, anger, melancholy, and avarice) and two are *carnal* (gluttony and lust). Like Cassian, he also described how each of these sins can act to spur on the other, as we noted before, not unlike a set of dominoes. We noted that Cassian described how gluttony leads to fornication,

Army of Deadly Sins

Avarice	Gluttony	Lust
Treachery	Foolish mirth	Blindness of mind
Fraud	Scurrility	Inconsiderateness
Deceit	Uncleanness	Inconstancy
Perjury	Babbling	Precipitousness
Restlessness	Dullness of sense in understanding	Self-love
Violence		Hatred of God
Hardness of heart against compassion		Affection for the present world
		Dread or despair of what is to come

which led to avarice, which leads to anger, which leads to sadness, which leads to acedia. In its own separate chain, he noted how vainglory leads to pride. Gregory provides two processions of his own, here using the term *offspring*, which would be capitalized later by St. Thomas Aquinas.

As for the spiritual vices, Gregory wrote that the first offspring of *pride* is *vainglory*. Because the corrupted, vainglorious mind seeks empty glory, it envies others who seek or obtain their own glory. *Envy*, in turn, generates *anger* when the mind is pierced by the internal wound of envy, and tranquillity is lost. When the mind strikes and harms itself by anger, *melancholy* ensues. When, due to grief and sadness, the soul obtains no joys from within, this sadness can beget *avarice* for external goods. As for the carnal sins, Gregory, like the theologians who came before him, also believed that *gluttony* sets the stage for *lust*. This idea may not be so plain to us today, but Gregory would write:

> But it is plain to all that lust springs from gluttony, when in the very distribution of the members, the genitals appear placed beneath the belly. And hence when the one is inordinately pampered, the other is doubtless excited to wantonness. (*Moralia*, XXXI, 89)

Gregory further analyzes the way these sins take hold of our souls and lead us from one to another by posing examples of questions each sin prompts us to ask ourselves. Here he is on envy:

> Envy is also wont to exhort the conquered heart, as if with reason, when it says, In what art thou inferior to this or that person? Why then art thou not either equal or superior to them? What great things art thou able to do, which they are not able to do! They ought not then to be either superior, or even equal, to thyself. (*Moralia*, XXXI, 90)

St. Thomas Aquinas, you'll recall, regarding the Church Fathers, was said to have inherited the intellect of them all. In our next chapter, the last one of our part I, we will see what his angelic intellect made of the great Patristic tradition of the seven deadly sins, and indeed, of their forty-four death-dealing daughters, as well.

CHAPTER 7

St. Thomas: The Seven Capital Vices and Their Death-Dealing Daughters

For the beginning of pride is sin, and the man who clings to it pours out abominations.

— SIRACH 10:13

For the love of money is the root of all evils; it is through this craving that some have wandered away from the faith and pierced their hearts with many pangs.

— 1 TIMOTHY 6:10

It would seem that no other special sins, besides pride and avarice, should be called capital.... On the contrary, Gregory (*Moral.* xxxi, 17) enumerates certain special vices under the name of capital.

— ST. THOMAS AQUINAS, *ST*, I-II, Q. 84, ART. 3

The Wise Man Puts Sins in Order

In the very first paragraph of his massive *Summa Contra Gentiles*, a summary of theology to be used in the conversion of non-Christians, St. Thomas Aquinas quotes "the Philosopher," the towering Aristotle of Stagira, Greece (384–322 B.C.), in stating the fundamental role of the philosopher as follows: "it belongs to the wise man to order."[35] Those who love (*philos*) wisdom (*sophia*) and are called wise are those who, according to Thomas "order things rightly and govern them well."[36] St. Thomas himself would go on to become among the most respected of philosophers and of theologians, one of the wisest men in the history of the Church and in the history of the world. The breadth of his knowledge was like a powerful searchlight, illuminating all within its reach, and the depth of his understanding was like a laser beam, penetrating deep into truths within the very heart of things. His wisdom was unsurpassed because he focused his mighty intellect first and foremost on God, who orders and governs all that is seen and unseen.

[35] St. Thomas Aquinas, *Summa Contra Gentiles*, trans. Anton C. Pegis (Notre Dame: IN: University of Notre Dame Press, 1955), 59.
[36] Ibid. In later sections, St. Thomas would make clear that the ultimate wisdom is seen in God, who orders and governs all that exists.

Fortunately for us, the light of St. Thomas's intellect did shine on the topic of the seven deadly sins within many places in his writings throughout the course of his career. St. Thomas, as a man who humbly sought wisdom, was not a man to seek novelty or innovation for its own sake, let alone to make a name for himself. His invaluable contributions to our study of the seven deadly sins come largely from his ability to order things, to make sense of the contributions of the great thinkers who came before him — from the divinely inspired authors of Scripture, to the Fathers and Doctors of the Church, to pagan Greek and Roman philosophers — to mine their brilliant insights for truth, to cultivate further the seeds of their great ideas, to reconcile real or apparent contradictions between them, and to organize and systematize a wealth of information in such a way that we can put it to use, to conquer sin within our souls and to glorify Him who gave us our souls in the first place.

This then is St. Thomas's great role in the history of the understanding of the seven deadly sins. He integrates and synthesizes virtually all the wisdom that came before him, and he shows us how to apply it. He does this within the context of sin in general — for example, in his book *De Malo* (*On Evil*). It is not until his eighth question, which is actually the eighth chapter halfway through his book, that St. Thomas addresses the deadly sins, "capital vices" in his language, for first he must address questions on evil, sins, the causes of sins, Original Sin, the punishment of Original Sin, human choice, and venial sin. Once he reaches the eighth question on the capital sins in general, almost all the rest of the book is devoted to this deadly topic, in the kind of breadth and depth for which St. Thomas is famous.

For example, when he begins to address whether there are seven capital sins, and whether they are the sins listed by Pope

St. Gregory the Great, he begins by presenting a full *two dozen* paragraph-long arguments *against* the idea that there are seven deadly sins, or that Gregory got the right ones! Only then does he present his opinion on the matter, and then he proceeds to answer all the arguments. Even in this book devoted to deadly sins, we will not dig in with such depth (although readers who might care to dig deeper are invited to dig up Thomas's *On Evil*, and by all means dive right on in!)

Fortunately for modern lay readers, St. Thomas has also provided a briefer, but still quite comprehensive examination of the seven deadly sins within his masterwork, the *Summa Theologica*. Our main focus then will be St. Thomas's treatment of the seven deadly sins within the second part of the *Summa Theologica*, which treats of man, who, through God's grace and the development of virtues, can move back toward the God who created him, this process made complete and perfect by Christ, the one Mediator and the true Way to God. As we move along, I'll let you know exactly where we are, in case you might like to dig deeper yourself.

Now, it's worth noting from the start that St. Thomas's main focus in his second part of the *Summa Theologica* was on things such as virtues, the gifts and fruits of the Holy Spirit, and the beatitudes, rather than on sin itself. These are glorious blessings that God would have us share. Thomas then was not nearly so interested in how low we can sink into sin and depravity as in how high we can rise toward God in virtue and grace. Sin still remained a highly important topic, though, because it is sins that prevent us from accepting and using God's grace, and developing glorious virtues within our souls.

Since we're speaking of order in this section, I'll note as well that St. Thomas discusses the deadly sins in different orders in *De Malo* and in the *Summa Theologica*. In this book, using the

THE SEVEN DEADLY SINS

St. Thomas's Treatments of the Seven Capital Vices

Summa Theologica	De Malo (On Evil)
The Seven Capital Vices in General I-II, Q. 84, art. 2	The Seven Capital Vices in General Q. 8, arts. 1–4
Sloth II-II, Q. 35, arts. 1–4	Vainglory Q. 9, arts. 1–3
Envy II-II, Q. 36, arts. 1–4	Envy Q. 10, arts. 1–3
Avarice II-II, Q. 118, arts. 1–8	Sloth Q. 11, arts. 1–4
Vainglory II-II, Q. 132, arts. 1–5	Wrath Q. 12. arts. 1–5
Gluttony II-II, Q. 148, arts. 1–5	Avarice Q. 13, arts. 1–4
Lust II-II, Q. 153, arts. 1–5	Gluttony Q. 14, arts. 1–4
Wrath II-II, Q. 158, arts. 1–8	Lust Q. 15, arts. 1–4

Summa Theologica's relatively terse presentation as our foundational guide, we will follow the order found there.

You'll recall that St. Thomas's primary focus in the second part of that book was to expound upon virtue and grace, and that theme would guide the order in which he presented the seven deadly sins. Each sin was addressed in the context of the theological, cardinal, and specific virtues it opposes. We'll explain that in depth in the chapters ahead, but for now, the chart on the opposite page will give you a peek.

**The Capital Vices and Contrary Virtues
in the *Summa Theologica***

Capital Vice	Contrary Specific Virtue	Contrary Theological or Cardinal Virtue
Sloth	Joy of charity about divine good	Charity
Envy	Joy of charity about our neighbor's good	Charity
Avarice	Liberality	Justice
Vainglory	Magnanimity	Fortitude
Gluttony	Abstinence	Temperance
Lust	Chastity	Temperance
Wrath	Meekness	Temperance

Let's lay out a few of St. Thomas's key themes on the concept of deadly sins in general, and in part II of this book, we'll try to mine his wisdom, worth its weight in spiritual gold.

Vice and Sin: What Are They — and Which One's Worse?

In contrasting the nature of virtue and sin, St. Thomas has noted that "sin does not consist in passing from the many to one, as is the case with virtues, which are connected, but rather in forsaking the one for the many."[37] Virtues seek out goods and ultimately the perfect good that is the original source and the final goal of all that is good — namely, God, of course. When we sin, we

[37] *ST*, I-II, Q. 73, art. 2.

forsake the ultimate goodness of God for the many lesser temporal goods we desire. God would have us love *ourselves*, but *after*, and *not contrary to* our love of Him and neighbor. When we sin, we declare that we love ourselves foremost. "Therefore it is evident that inordinate love of self is the cause of every sin."[38]

So sin is *caused* by a self-love in which we turn toward things of the world and away from God. Sin is *manifested* in thoughts (or desires), words, or deeds, and in that they may be seen as three degrees or stages of sin. For example: "For the angry man, through desire of vengeance, is at first disturbed in thought, then he breaks out into words of abuse, and lastly he goes on to wrongful deeds; and the same applies to lust or any other sin."[39]

But what about *vice*? Thomas informs us that "Augustine says (*De Perfect. Just.* 2) that vice is a quality in respect of which the soul is evil," and further, "(*De Lib. Arb.* 3): Whatever is lacking for a thing's natural perfection may be called a vice."[40] Thomas notes that as virtues are habits that make a person good, vices are habits that dispose us toward evil—evil being the lack of good. Vices are bad or evil habits, as virtues are good habits. Sins are vicious acts (literally, acts of vice). Sins are to vices as good deeds are to virtues.

So which one's worse, vice or sin? Well, to make a long story short—*sin*. Thomas says, "A man is justly punished for a vicious act; but not for a vicious habit, so long as no act ensues. Therefore a vicious action is worse than a vicious habit."[41] It is a bad thing to develop a habit disposing oneself toward evil,

[38] *ST*, I-II, Q. 77, art. 4.
[39] *ST*, I-II, Q. 72, art. 7.
[40] *ST*, I-II, Q. 71, art. 1.
[41] *ST*, I-II, Q. 72, art. 3.

but a worse thing to exercise one's will to act upon it. Indeed, by repeatedly choosing *not* to act on vicious habits, vices may be diminished.

Our take-home lesson for this Thomistic distinction between vice and sin is that St. Thomas classifies our seven deadly sins more precisely as seven deadly *vices*, as ingrained *habits* disposing us toward acts of sin if we do not act to conquer those vicious habits and to replace them with virtuous ones. Virtues perfect us, making us and our actions good. Vices destroy the spark of God within us, leading us toward sin. What kind of habits do *you* want to build? *What kind of person do you want to be?* If it is goodness you seek, and the evil of sin that you seek to avoid, then the seven capital vices should become your deadly enemies.

Deadlier Sins Than the Seven Deadly Sins?

In laying the groundwork for his defense and explanation of St. Gregory's delineation of the seven capital vices, St. Thomas also addresses arguments arising from the Scripture passages that we used at the start of this chapter. We saw that St. Paul tells us, "The desire of money is the root of all evils" (1 Tim. 6:10). Thomas explains that as roots provide the nourishment that a noxious vine needs to thrive and grow, so does covetousness seek riches that can provide means for someone to satisfy his desire for other sins. This is not to say that covetousness is the *only* root of evils, since other sins, such as ambition or gluttony, might lead a person toward *avarice* (another name for covetousness) for money. But other evils *more frequently* arise from the love of money.

As we saw in our second quotation at this chapter's start, we learn from Scripture that "the beginning of pride is sin" (Sir.

The Seven Capital Vices and Their Forty-Four

Sloth	Envy	Avarice	Vainglory
II-II, 35, 4	II-II, 36, 4	II-II, 118, 8	II-II,132, 5
Malice	Hatred	Treachery	Disobedience
Spite	Tale-bearing	Fraud	Boastfulness
Faintheartedness	Detraction	Falsehood	Hypocrisy
Despair	Joy at another's misfortune	Perjury	Contention
Sluggish-ness about the Commandments	Grief at another's prosperity	Restlessness	Obstinacy
Wandering of the mind after unlawful things		Violence	Discord
		Insensitivity to mercy	Eccentricity

10:13).[42] Thomas notes that pride, in the sense of an inordinate desire to excel, *is* the beginning of sin. A covetous person, for instance, might desire to acquire all temporal goods so that through them he may have some perfection or excellence. In this case, St. Thomas tells us, "pride, which is the desire to excel,

[42] The book of Sirach is cited as "Ecclus." for Ecclesiasticus in St. Thomas's writings.

Death-Dealing Daughters in the *Summa Theologica*

Gluttony II-II, 148, 6	Lust II-II, 153, 5	Wrath II-II, 158,8
Unseemly joy	Blindness of mind	Quarreling
Scurrility	Thoughtlessness	Swelling of the mind
Uncleanness	Inconstancy	Contumely
Loquaciousness	Rashness	Clamor
Dullness of mind	Self-love	Indignation
	Hatred of God	Blasphemy
	Love of the world	
	Abhorrence and despair of a future world	

is said to be the beginning of sin." But covetousness is said to be the root of all evils because it furnishes "the opportunity of fulfilling all desires of sin."[43]

As we soon will see, while recognizing the instrumental power of avarice or covetousness as a means to bringing other sins to fulfillment, it is to *pride* that St. Thomas, like St. Gregory before

[43] *ST*, I-II, Q. 84, art. 2.

him, gives pride of place, as more capital, we might say, with a capital C, than the seven capital sins. Pride provides not only the *means*, but the ultimate *end* that sins seek out.

Pride, though, we might say, is far too proud to soil its hands with all of the dirty detail work involved in engendering sin. It delegates those seven deadly "captains," the seven deadly vices as St. Thomas calls them, to serve its sinful ends. Those captains, as we saw in Gregory's treatment, are active and virile, engendering forty-four "daughters." Let's take our first look at what Thomas made of those death-dealing daughters.

The Forty-Four Decadent, Death-Dealing Daughters

In the *Summa Theologica*, when addressing each of the seven capital vices, Thomas notes how many "daughters" Gregory, in his *Moralia* on the book of Job has "assigned" to each capital vice, before addressing each of those "daughters."[44] Gregory had depicted the deadly vices as military captains, but he also addressed the sins that followed them as their "offspring." We saw the familial metaphor and mention of fathers, mothers, and daughters used dramatically by St. John Climacus in his *Ladder of Divine Ascent*. If sins can have fathers, they likely could have sons, just as well, but St. Thomas has carried on the traditional rendering of "daughters" for the sins that flow from and feed into the capital vices. Perhaps this is partly because the word *daughters* especially suggests the fecundity of these related vices,

---

[44] At times, Thomas also notes daughters of capital vices enumerated by another influential Catholic theologian and Doctor of the Church, St. Isidore (560–636), Archbishop of Seville, Spain, a man dubbed by the nineteenth-century historian Montalembert as "the last scholar of the ancient world."

of their capacity to give birth to new generations of vices and sins, so to speak; sins whose family histories may be traced back to the capital vices.

On the following page you can take a glimpse at these deadly daughters right now. We'll get to know them better as we examine each one in the chapters of part II.

Vice and Sin Go Global

We saw how the concept of listing and examining "deadly sins" sprung up in the deserts of the East and spread to the monasteries of the West as well. As a child, St. Thomas spent years with the Benedictine monks of Monte Casino, Italy, and as an adult Dominican friar, he would head northwest to the University of Paris to do some of his most notable mature work. He studied, prayed, and taught as well in other places too, including Cologne, Germany, and Naples, Italy. Within a century of his death, St. Thomas had come to be called the Common Doctor of the Church, a man for all of Christ's Church that spans all the nations of the world and all the eons of time. St. Thomas's insights are relevant across the globe and across the ages. The seven deadly sins and their death-dealing daughters, unfortunately for our souls, are still alive and kicking everywhere. In part II we'll borrow from him and from those who came before him and after him, to learn how we can put these sins in their place, a place far from our souls.

Before we dive into part II, let's review where we've been so far.[45]

---

[45] Along with a preview of where we'll eventually go, with the rendering of the seven capital sins within our modern-day *Catechism of the Catholic Church*.

A Family History of Deadly, Capital, Cardinal, Thoughts, Sins, and Vices

Evagrius Eight Evil Thoughts	St. John Cassian Eight Principal Vices	Prudentius Seven Vices	St. John Climacus Seven Sinful Passions	Pope St. Gregory Seven Capital Sins	St. Thomas Seven Capital Vices	Catechism of the Catholic Church Seven Capital Sins
Gluttony	Gluttony	Idolatry	Gluttony	Vainglory	Vainglory	Pride
Fornication	Fornication	Lust	Lust	Anger	Wrath	Avarice
Avarice	Avarice	Wrath	Avarice	Envy	Envy	Envy
Distress	Anger	Pride	Despondency	Melancholy	Sloth	Wrath
Anger	Sadness	Indulgence	Anger	Avarice	Avarice	Lust
Akedia	Acedia	Greed	Vainglory	Gluttony	Gluttony	Gluttony
Vanity	Vainglory	Discord	Pride	Lust	Lust	Sloth or acedia

Battle Plans to Decimate Deadly Vice and Sin

For though we walk in the flesh, we do not war according to the flesh. For the weapons of our warfare are not carnal, but mighty to God unto the pulling down of fortifications, destroying counsels, and every height that exalteth itself against the knowledge of God, and bringing into captivity every understanding unto the obedience of Christ.

2 CORINTHIANS 10:3–5

Prologue to Part II

"Those who don't know history are condemned to repeat it," goes a saying attributed to eighteenth-century political philosopher Edmund Burke. Well, now we know the history of the seven deadly sins, so it's time to try to make sure that we don't repeat them within our own lives!

We will seek now to turn contemplation into action as we devise battle plans to conquer those deadly sins and to grow in the spiritual life of our souls. Although I am certainly unable to advise anyone from the perspective of one who has conquered these sins himself, I do stand ready to point you to the strategies and arm you with some of the weapons that great saints have devised to assist us in our relentless struggles against sin, toward virtue, and ultimately, toward union with God. We will dip into the arsenals of those great Desert Fathers, the early Doctors of the Church, St. Thomas Aquinas, and a vast company of great sages and saints who have graced the earth (and heaven) up until our time.

Borrowing from St. John Climacus, and from St. Thomas Aquinas as well, we will feature a metaphorical ladder in our battle plan against the deadly sins. You will recall from chapter 5 Climacus's *Ladder of Divine Ascent*, upon which we may climb away from sin and toward virtue (if we accept the boosts of God's grace).

St. Thomas has also employed a metaphor for growth in spiritual perfection that may suggest a ladder. In describing the three fundamental stages of spiritual perfection as the *avoidance of sin* consuming the effort of beginners, *the pursuit of virtue* claiming the focus of proficients along the way, and the *union with and enjoyment of God* as the focus of the perfect, he observes that even the proficients in pursuit of virtue at step two of the ladder are never completely free from sin. They must also continue to fight the good fight against their sinful natures. Thomas quite graphically compares this task to the work of those who built the walls of Jerusalem while fighting off their enemies, who "with one hand labored on the work and with the other held up his weapon" (Neh. 4:17).

Let us then imagine those builders of Jerusalem up on their ladders, building up the walls. Let this be the image of our ladder—a ladder upon which we will fight against sin as we climb toward virtue. We seek to conquer the seven deadly sins, and so our ladder will have seven steps. At each of these steps we will find general, fundamental strategies we can apply to wage battle against any deadly sin and its daughters. I'll simply list them now and will explain and apply them in our last seven chapters as they pertain to each one of the seven deadly sins.

Seven Steps toward Conquering the Seven Deadly Sins
1. Examination of conscience
2. Embracing the sacraments
3. Watching the steps of our movements toward sin
4. Practicing prayer
5. Cultivating virtue
6. Immersion in the world of the spirit
7. Imitation of Christ

CHAPTER 8

Slashing Sloth

"You there! You crass and sluggish creature.... Who
are your enemies? Who can destroy you?" And
tedium may be constrained to reply ... "The singing of psalms and manual labor are my opponents
by whom I am now bound. My enemy is the thought
of death, but what really slays me is prayer backed
by a firm hope in the blessings of the future."

— ST. JOHN CLIMACUS,
THE LADDER OF DIVINE ASCENT

We have made a religion of ourselves
and, of all the sins, we have come near-
est to making a religion of Sloth.

— **HENRY FAIRLIE,** *THE SEVEN DEADLY SINS*[46]

---

[46] Henry Fairlie, *The Seven Deadly Sins Today* (Notre
Dame, IN: University of Notre Dame Press, 1979),
129.

Are You Ready to Sleuth Sloth from the
Ancient Hermit's Cell to the Modern Living Room?

In the sixth century, Climacus wrote of the spiritual apathy of acedia, or sloth, as a dread opponent of isolated monks seeking a mystical union with God. In the 1970s, Fairlie wrote of sloth as a popular false god, enshrined by a modern culture in which so many have lost all notion of devotion to God, replaced by absorption in the self. Although our culture, especially in its values and its technology, has clearly changed in the course of those many centuries, human nature has not changed much. Sloth, although manifest in some new ways, is still as deadly as ever, yet it is also clearly still alive and well.

"Tedium," said Climacus, "is a paralysis of the soul, a slackness of mind, a neglect of religious exercises, a hostility to vows taken. It is an approval of worldly things."[47] The desert monk afflicted by the "noonday demon" of acedia will become bored by his prayers, will feel fatigue and weakness, will feel like leaning while standing and like sitting while leaning. Acedia will lead to distractions; at the slightest noise the hermit will look out his window. Sloth may lead him to think of good deeds he might do, to go out and visit others, perhaps bringing them

---

[47] St. John Climacus, *The Ladder of Divine Assent*, 162.

87

solace. Christ did tell us to visit the sick, after all (Matt. 25:36). Sloth may also lead him to remember the pleasures of his past life in the world and whisper to him that his work and prayer are fruitless and futile.

Not many of us today spend our days in a cell in the desert, but are there not many ways in which we too are beset by the ancient noonday demon of sloth—indeed, at any hour of the day? Don't we feel disinclined at times to do the important tasks we know we should do, be it in our homes, at work, in our prayer life, or for the needs of the Church? Don't we sometimes feel an apathy or listlessness that leads to slothful idleness?

On the other hand, aren't many of us living lives with no time or room for idleness, packed with so much work and so many extracurricular hobbies, commitments, and various activities that we "don't have time to think" (let alone to pray)? Sloth is not merely the sin slouching next to the couch potato, gazing at the giant flat-screen TV, munching chips. True spiritual sloth is just as happy to work up a sweat, spurring on the workaholic to work his fingers to the bone seven days a week, helping the boisterously enthusiastic sports fan become ever more "fan-atic," leaving other concerns in the lurch, encouraging the fitness buff to devote ever more time to become more buff and more sleek, leaving it to other less dynamic souls to just sit there in some church.

So what can we do about this deadly sin of sloth known by so many names,[48] expressed by so many diverse and diverting actions and avoidance of actions? Let's take a step onto the first

---

[48] Such as acedia, despondency, tedium, apathy, sorrow, laziness, indolence, to name but a few. See also Wicked Word #1 in appendix A.

rung of our ladder to gather our first weapon, to battle the many-headed serpent of the capital vice of sloth.

Examining Sloth in the Light of Noonday

An essential first step in any battle is to know one's enemy. St. Thomas Aquinas noted that St. John Damascene described sloth as "an oppressive sorrow" that weighs down a man's mind (or a woman's, of course) so that he wants to do nothing. It does lead then to a particular kind of laziness regarding spiritual things. Sloth is "a sluggishness of the mind which neglects to do good."[49]

Sloth, this spiritual apathy, sadness, or sorrow, can be evil both *in itself* and *in its effects*. Sloth is evil *in itself* because it is sadness in reaction not to something evil, but to the highest of goods, the spiritual goods of God. Sloth is evil *in its effects* when it keeps us from performing acts of good. This is why the Apostle (St. Paul) "(2 Cor. 2:7) did not wish those who repented to be *swallowed up with overmuch sorrow*." Because sloth is both evil in itself and in its effects, Thomas declares it is truly a sin. So what are we going to do about it?

Socrates famously said that "the unexamined life is not worth living" and he went about asking other questions to help people examine the truly important things in life and the extent to which they understood them and sought them out in their actions. We call his practice of questions and answers the *dialectical* or Socratic method. We saw it at its historical pin-nacle in medieval times in the formalized question-and-answer, objection-and-reply method of works such as Thomas's *Summa Theologica*.

[49] Quotations in this section are from *ST*, II-II, Q. 35, art. 1.

In a less formal sense, we can apply this method to ourselves in our daily lives, asking questions of ourselves that will make our potential slothful ideas, emotions, and actions (or inactions) conscious as we examine our conscience. Having learned that sloth is *a spiritual apathy, a sadness or boredom about the divine good of God*, we can ask ourselves to what extent have we invited this demon (or at least this vice) into the chambers of our hearts. The fact that you are reading this book suggests that you already have a thirst for spiritual things, unless perhaps you have picked it up out of boredom with prayer or scriptural reading!

Still, do you feel at times like one of the "lukewarm," "neither hot nor cold," that God will spit out of His mouth? (cf. Rev. 3:16). Are you merely going through the motions in your spiritual life or finding it hard to muster the effort even to go through those motions? Do you find yourself restless, constantly feeling the need for some diversion, checking your phone for e-mail or the latest social blurb or link on social media? You've seen it or done it. I've seen couples or pairs of friends at restaurants, facing and interacting not with each other, but with the glowing little screens in their hands. Can't they rest content in the company of the spouse or the friend God has given them? St. Augustine knew what he was talking about when he said to God, "Our hearts are restless until they rest in Thee." Is this why people today are so restless and seeking constant diversions? Are we not content to rest in God, and is this due to sloth?

Those death-dealing daughters that so deftly serve sloth can help us examine our conscience as well. They can also help us examine the cultural trends and events that might encourage us toward sloth. We can ask ourselves probing questions guided by targeting these daughters.

- Are there ways that I become *sluggish regarding the Commandments?*[50] Do I keep holy the Lord's Day, go to Mass, and happily rest in God?

- Does my mind *wander after unlawful things?* Am I so apathetic about the things of God that I am easily enticed away from devotional practices and Christian virtue by petty or sinful diversions? As Aristotle stated, "Those who find no joy in spiritual pleasures have recourse to pleasures of the body." Am I one of those? Do I see this in the members of my family? Have I given them an example of one who takes joy in spiritual pleasures?

- Am I *fainthearted* regarding my spiritual obligations? Have I asked God for the courage and fortitude to do difficult things?

- Do I succumb at times to the spirit of *despair?* Do I lose hope in the joy that God has in store for me and my loved ones? Do I doubt His power and mercy?

- Have I felt or evidenced *spite* toward those who lead others to spiritual goods? Have I been angered at Church leaders who dare to speak out against emerging cultural trends that distort and devalue the dignity of human life or the sanctity of marriage? To what extent have I submitted to Caesar the things that are truly God's, aiding

---

[50] Do you even *know* the Ten Commandments? They're in Exodus 20:2–17 and Deuteronomy 5:6–21 and spelled out in the *Catechism* in paragraphs 2051 and 2052. A simple method to learn them literally forward and backward in just a few minutes, borrowing from St. Thomas Aquinas, is found in chapter 1 of my *Memorize the Faith!*

and abetting God's enemies, in spreading spiritual sloth throughout our land?

• Am I ever tempted toward *malice*, to detest the spiritual goods of God? We can see explicit malice at work in our time in the writings of the "new atheists," who have moved beyond disagreement with those who hold to the reality of God's existence to an active and vitriolic hatred of religion and the things of God. We may love God dearly in our hearts, but do we take any action to counter such malice, by speaking out for God's truth and evidencing God's love even to those who persecute us — and Him?

Why Even Sloth Runs from the Sacraments

The seven sacraments that Christ gave to the Church are all very powerful weapons in the battle against deadly sins, prompting even sloth to sprint off to hide. Baptism makes us members of the mighty Body of Christ, and Confirmation fortifies us to fight the good fight as mature Christian soldiers. It is Confession, however, the sacrament of Reconciliation, that is the step that most explicitly follows upon an examination of our conscience. It is the next rung up our ladder. After we have shined the light upon the sins of sloth within our souls, it is the optimal time to seek from God their absolution and the grace to continue to fight them. When we give up those sins, our union with God is restored.

The very act of going to Confession is one against spiritual apathy and a turning of our heart toward God. Sloth says, "God, I don't care." Confession says, "O my God, I am heartily sorry for having offended Thee." When we express our sins of spiritual apathy, Christ will indeed forgive them through the priest, by supplying us with grace and prescribing acts of penance and practical advice we can use in our battles against sloth and its daughters.

Watching the Lumbering Steps of Sloth

Our third step up the ladder away from sloth, following examination of our conscience and embracing the sacrament of Confession, is that of *watching the steps of our movements toward the sin of sloth*. Pop quiz: Do you recall St. John Climacus's six steps in the process of our movements toward sin? I don't expect that you do, so here is the answer key:

1. Provocation
2. Coupling
3. Assent
4. Captivity
5. Struggle
6. Passion

Now let's look at them one by one, as they relate to the vice of sloth.

1. *Provocation.* Breaking down the internal and external stimuli toward sins and the steps of their development within our souls can help us better combat them. Climacus builds on the writings of Stoic philosophers and Desert Fathers such as Evagrius, who stressed that vices can begin as fleeting "first movements," or "proto-passions," that can strike us in an instant as natural reactions of beings with bodily senses and appetites that are not under the complete control of our wills. St. Thomas was well aware of the "sensitive" powers of our souls that we share with

lower animals. Our sensations can prompt reflexive reactions in us, as the sight of food might make a hungry man salivate, or a fleeting pornographic image might trigger the beginnings of a physiological response affecting hormones and blood flow without our willful intention. Modern biologists and neuroscientists would associate such reactions to lower-brain centers in man, but they are also to some extent controllable in their progression by man's higher powers of reason.

These initial reactions are not always necessarily sinful of themselves. Thomas calls them "first movements," and in Climacus's steps, they are called *provocation*. For some deadly sins, these provocations may be felt much more quickly or intensely than for others. The provocations toward sloth may be subtle, as the desert fathers described in the experience of desert monks coping with acedia. Perhaps the monk sees or hears something or maybe even smells an aroma, perhaps of food or perfume, and recalls an image of a time in his past life when he enjoyed a simple sensual pleasure. This image has now, per Climacus, entered into the monk's heart. That recollection itself was instantaneous and not sinful. But what will our monk do with it?

2. *Coupling* is that conversation we have within ourselves regarding that word or image of provocation, either with or without passion. This stage may be sinful, depending on what we have to say to ourselves and the way we say it. Does our monk thank God for the memory of that simple pleasure and return to his task, or does he nurse it, let it divert him from his task, and perhaps focus his attention on how he can experience the likes of it again?

3. *Assent*, as we saw before in chapter 5, can be best expressed in the words (translated) of Climacus himself: "the delighted yielding of the soul to what it has encountered.... The condition of

the soul determines whether or not the third is sinful." So, has the monk yielded to that thought of pleasure and drunk it in with delight? Was that yielding sinful? It depends on the nature of the thought itself and on the state of the monk's soul. Was the remembered experience a sinful one? Has the monk assented to allow an evil to remain in his heart?

4. *Captivity* is "a forcible and unwilling abduction of the heart, a permanent lingering with what we have encountered and which totally undermines the necessary order of our souls." Captivity is judged for its sinfulness in terms of the situation (such as whether it occurs at prayer or at other times) and its subject matter (such as whether it is in regards to something trivial or "in the context of evil thoughts"). So then, has the thought our monk consented to taken hold of his soul? Has he rendered himself captive to a captain of deadly sins?

5. *Struggle* refers to the internal resistance, or lack thereof, against the building attack on the soul; to whether one marshals sufficient power of the soul to counter the attack or whether one succumbs to the pleasures of desire. So then, when our monk sees that his soul has been captivated by slothful thoughts, does he muster his strength to break free? Does he ask God to provide him with strength?

6. *Passion* is the result of a lost struggle that may remain hidden within the soul but acts to become like a habit, until the soul clings to it of its own will, indeed, "with affection." Passion, says Climacus, is always denounced as sin and calls for either repentance or future punishment. If our monk has not mustered his strength and called on the strength of God, and his struggle is lost, he has allowed his thoughts to give birth to a bad habit,

indeed, to a capital vice — in this case, the vice of acedia or sloth. Soon it will give birth to its six death-dealing daughters, as the monk experiences the spiritual deadness that comes from abandoning the joy of the goodness of God in pursuit of far lesser goods.

We must recall, of course, that the steps of this process are not unique to our fourth- or fifth-century desert monk but apply every day to you and me as well. If we are to battle sin and win (with God's grace) we will attune ourselves to steps like these within the workings of our own souls. Our best bet is to follow the sound and wise advice of the sometimes silly and foolish Deputy Barney Fife of the old *Andy Griffith Show*, namely, to "Nip it in the bud. Nip-it-in-the-bud!" We'll have practice aplenty in the chapters ahead, and we need not always be aware of all of these six steps, but if we do become more aware of the general process in which the temptation toward sin and the movement from thoughts to desires to deeds unfold within our souls, we will be far better armed to battle vice and sin and to nip them in the bud, as soon as we become aware of them and before they bear sour fruits in our hearts.

Prayer and Sloth Are Like Oil and Water

So we ascend now to the fourth rung of our ladder away from the vice of spiritual sloth, and here we find one of the most powerful armaments known to the desert fathers and every bit as powerful and useful to all of us today. Recall from Climacus's quotation at the start of this chapter that personified sloth itself declares that singing of psalms and manual labor bind him, and his enemy is thoughts of death, but what really "slays" him is "prayer backed by a firm hope in the blessings of the future." Prayer and sloth just don't mix, but let's look at all of the parts of sloth's confession.

The singing of psalms is, of course, a form of prayer that was at the heart of the prayer life of hermits and monks in the times of Evagrius, Climacus, Gregory, and Thomas, as it remains in our own day. Sloth is an indifference or apathy toward divine things and God, but the psalms immerse us in our relationship with God, expressing confidence in His guidance and goodness, and expressing our gratitude and praise.

Ora et labora, prayer and work, were the heart of monastic life. Not only does prayer mix poorly with sloth, but work does as well. Spiritual sloth may indeed be expressed in physical indolence, sluggishness, and downright laziness, when we simply don't care enough to honor God in even the most menial of our tasks. To train ourselves to love our labors, and to "pray always" as we do them, is to train ourselves to experience and relish the spiritual joys born of charity.

Recall too that Climacus called sloth's enemy "the thought of death." We would do well to ask ourselves if we think of death often enough. Do we remind ourselves we are but wayfarers on earth, "ashes to ashes, dust to dust," on our way toward those four last things: death, judgment, heaven, and hell? If we do not bear this in mind, we may become susceptible to sloth as our minds wander after temporal things, having forgotten about what's eternal.

Our main focus here, though, is on that "prayer backed by a firm hope in the blessings of the future." Pray has been called a turning of the heart and a rising of the mind toward God. In this sense it is an almost instant remedy to the spiritual apathy of sloth, even if we should become distracted in our prayer or do not experience an emotional high from it. It still shows that we care enough to pray. If we can also back our prayers with a "firm hope" in the blessings God will bestow on us in the future, then we can also remove ourselves from spiritual sadness and climb toward the joys of union with God, the source, sustainer, and goal of our hope.

So then, what shall you do to combat sloth with prayer? Does even the thought of the time, energy, and focus required of the Divine Office or the Holy Rosary leave you with feelings of listlessness and fatigue? Then why not start with simple prayers? Even a prayer as short and simple as the Sign of the Cross, if prayed with an earnest heart, can start to send sloth into retreat. Indeed, some of the most zealous saints prayed it and signed it many times throughout each day. It is hard to let your mind wander after unlawful things when you are repeatedly praying that all of your thoughts, word, and deeds may be done, "in the name of the Father, and of the Son, and of the Holy Spirit. Amen." Further, you can pray in your own simple words as well, specifically asking God to help you to conquer the vice of sloth.

Surprising Sloth by Joy and Her Virtuous Comrades in Arms

Vice and sin miss the targets we were made for by under- or over-shooting the mark, while virtues hit the bull's-eye. As Prudentius made clear with dramatic flair centuries ago, we can also use virtues to target deadly vices. Sloth, said Thomas, opposes the virtue of *charity*, and specifically the *joy* that should flow from charity *regarding the divine Good*. God gives us so much that is good, starting with our very existence, and promises so much more, that to allow ourselves to become mired in sloth would also seem the height of *ingratitude*. "Sure, God, you're the source of every good that I've ever had or will have," says sloth, "but what have you done for me lately?"

Sloth is also a very self-centered vice in that it consumes the very self we seek to serve by it. We see it in modern cravings for experience, in that *seeking after unlawful things*, because our hearts are no longer moved by the true, the good, and the beautiful. Many now boldly and openly seek instead the easy highs, such as those that can come from ceaseless entertainment, from drugs, or from casual sexual acts. Indeed, when the things people desire are contrary to God's law as embodied in millennia of civilization's positive, manmade laws, many now seek not only to disregard those laws, but indeed, to abolish them.[51]

So what kind of virtues can we strive to develop to conquer sloth? Well actually, there are many. *Diligence* is a virtue directly opposed to the physical manifestations of sloth such as idleness or laziness, since it basically means the habit of doing hard work. Habits are built by practice, so the physically slothful need to cultivate the virtue of diligence in repeated bouts of meaningful effort, however small they may need to be at first. Those who would cultivate diligence should well be aware that all work can be meaningful and can serve to glorify God. "In all toil there is profit" (Prov. 14:23).

And what other virtues can inspire us to build diligence in our souls?

- *Gratitude* is a good one for starters; we should avoid taking for granted the good gifts from God, by practicing

---

[51] At the time I write, prominent examples include the push for the legalization of recreational marijuana and of so-called same-sex marriage. "If it feels good do it" is the unquestioned wisdom in many political circles today and tough luck for the "bigots" who question it and for those will be harmed by making lawful illicit self-indulgence.

prayers of thanksgiving and expressing our gratitude to those who do good deeds or take care of us.

- *Piety* is another way to develop diligence. It gives God special reverence, not only as the Creator, or even the Sustainer of our existence, but as our *Father*.

- *Religion* is a virtue that Thomas treats under the cardinal virtue of *justice*. Justice involves giving another his rightful due. God has given us so much that we can never give Him back his rightful due in equal measure, but we can return to Him what is within our power by practicing the virtue of religion through the various internal acts of contemplation and mental prayers, as well as in external acts of worship, almsgiving, and more.

When we strive to build virtues such as diligence, gratitude, piety, and religion in our hearts, and ask God to help us do so, even during periods of dryness or apathy, even when it is not easy to do, we may again find the joy that comes from the virtue of charity surging once more through our souls.

Immerse Yourself in the World of the Spirit, and Sloth Will Slither Away

The carnal world, the world of the flesh, has always presented powerful temptations to draw us away from the things of God. In our modern electronic, virtual world there are more places for our minds to wander than ever before, and it is harder than ever to rest content with any one of them. There is always one more channel to surf, one more social-media entry to peruse, one more link to click. When it comes to finding meaning and contentment, it seems we are always striving and never arriving. So often too, we are consumed in the pursuit of the banal, the trivial, the lurid, and the ugly, as we grow numb to the true, the good, and the beautiful. How then can we raise our minds and hearts to the higher things of the spiritual life and keep them from becoming mired in the mud of spiritual apathy?

It is our senses that typically lead us away from our relationship with God, but we have the capacity to harness those senses and to put them to good use by the powers of reason God has given us. Yes, we are influenced by our environments, but we also have the capacity to control, to some extent, the environments that we place ourselves in. If we are to conquer spiritual sloth, we need to harness our senses and arrange our environments so that we regularly receive the spiritual tonic that can come from the true, the good, and the beautiful.

We are strongly influenced by the images we see, so what kind of images are we going to seek out? Many are drawn to Christ and the Catholic Church by the moving power of great religious art throughout the ages, from the paintings of Fra Angelico, to the sculptures of Michelangelo, to the uplifting architectural majesty of the great Gothic cathedrals. Those of us already in the Church may find our sloth slithering away if we take some time to seek out and reflect upon such holy works of beauty.

We know too that "faith comes from what is heard" (Rom. 10:17). So what have you been hearing lately? Do you listen to radio programs or music that draw you toward heaven or that mire you in the earth? Much of today's most popular music has become explicitly vile and vulgar in a way hardly imagined just a few decades ago, yet genres of music have existed for ages that can combat our sloth and draw up our minds to the beauty and glory of God. The name of one of our greatest authorities on the seven deadly sins is also associated with some of the most moving and reverent sounds that have been heard for many centuries. I refer, of course, to Gregorian chant, a beautiful aid to meditation and prayer. If you have an ear for classical music, are you aware that most of the greatest of the classical composers have composed beautiful Masses? Perhaps you're familiar with Mozart's dramatically stunning Requiem Mass (a favorite with Hollywood movie producers), but have you heard the Masses of Beethoven or of Bruckner or the Orthodox Liturgies of St. John Chrysostom by Rachmaninoff or Tchaikovsky? They are waiting there on CD or on the Internet to help shake us from our sloth and set our ears and our hearts toward higher things.

The full verse of Romans 10:17 goes, "So faith comes from what is heard, and what is heard comes by the preaching of Christ." To immerse in the spiritual world then, we must hear the word of Christ. We do this with other members of Christ's Body in the context of the Mass, and we should also read the Gospels and other books of Scripture regularly at home, if we are to conquer spiritual apathy. Indeed, why not try using some of the great chants or classical liturgical pieces as a reverential, moving backdrop for your prayer or spiritual reading? (I must confess that they are great inspiration for spiritual *writing* as well!)

Note well too that Evagrius himself once wrote a complete book, the *Antirrhetikos*, or *Talking Back*, that explains how to cite scriptural verses to combat each of his "eight assailing thoughts." Here is a small sample of the fifty-seven verses he recommends for "talking back" to sloth (acedia):

- ◆ Genesis 3:19: "In the sweat of your face / you shall eat bread / till you return to the ground, / for out of it you were taken; / you are dust, / and to dust you shall return."

- Numbers 13:21: "So they went up and spied out the land from the wilderness of Zin to Rehob, near the entrance of Hamath."

- Deuteronomy: 6:4–5: "Hear, O Israel: The LORD our God is one LORD; and you shall love the LORD your God with all your heart, and with all your soul, and with all your might."

- Psalm 33:2: "Praise the Lord with the lyre, / make melody to him with the harp of ten strings!"

- Philippians 1:29–30: "For it has been granted to you that for the sake of Christ you should not only believe in him but also suffer for his sake, engaged in the same conflict which you saw and now hear to be mine."

- James 1:2–4, 12: "Count it all joy, my brethren, when you meet various trials, for you know that the testing of your faith produces steadfastness. And let steadfastness have its full effect, that you may be perfect and complete, lacking in nothing. Blessed is the man who endures trial, for when he has stood the test he will receive the crown of life which God has promised to those who love him."

Smell and touch are other senses we might enlist to help in the battle against sloth. Do you ever literally stop to smell the flowers and to thank God for providing them? Does incense draw your thoughts toward God? If so, consider using some in your own devotional practices at home.

If successful, practices like these will help to still our restless hearts and to reclaim some of the joy that comes from charity. But by the very nature of charity, that joy will not be self-absorbed, a joy that is all about us. It will inflame our hearts to care for our neighbor as well, as our focus moves away from gratifying our petty wants to glorifying God and loving our neighbor through Him.

See Christ on the Cross and Sloth Disappears

During Lent of 1939 Venerable Archbishop Fulton J. Sheen gave a fascinating series of radio addresses in which he related each of the seven deadly sins to Christ's seven last words on the Cross.[52] As we ascend to the seventh and last rung of our spiritual ladder, let's imagine we've reached the top of our wall and from it we spy the most moving scene in the universe, for there hangs Christ on His Cross on Calvary. As followers of Christ, we are to love Him and to strive to imitate Him. As He hung on the Cross, we should strive to hang on to every word that comes from His mouth.

Which of Christ's "seven last words" on the Cross did Sheen associate with sloth? "It is finished" (John 19:30). Those words that He uttered before He bowed His head and gave up His spirit make clear that Christ had work to do on earth—and so do we, if we are to take up our cross and follow Him. We are to be "doers of the word, and not hearers only" (James 1:22). Our faith must be enlivened by charity and flow into good works. "It is not enough for the student to have faith in the teacher's knowledge, he must also study."[53] It is up to us to study Christ and to strive to

---

[52] See appendix B for a summary of the traditional seven last words and Sheen's linkage of them to the seven deadly sins.
[53] Fulton J. Sheen, *The Seven Capital Sins* (New York: Alba House, 2001), 68.

grow to be like Him. If we can imagine that the seventh step of our ladder has brought us to the feet of the Christ crucified and remember that He suffered and died so that our sins would be conquered and the gates that lead to eternal joy would be opened, we can stand well armed against the most weary, mundane, and unimaginative vice of sloth and all her death-dealing daughters.

CHAPTER 9

Ending Envy

When you envy the virtue of another you are your own greatest enemy; for if you continue in a state of grace, united to your neighbor through charity, you have a share in all his good works, and the more he merits the richer you become. So far, therefore, from envying his virtue, you should find it a source of consolation. Alas! Because your neighbor is advancing, will you fall back? Ah! If you would love him in the virtues which you do not find in yourself, you would share in them through charity; the profit of his labors would also become yours.

—VENERABLE LOUIS OF GRANADA,
THE SINNER'S GUIDE[54]

---

[54] Louis of Granada, *The Sinner's Guide* (Veritas Splendor Publications, 2012), 289.

Are You Green (or Blue) with Envy?

We are all prone to the vice of envy, and yet few of us really want those blues that come from being green with envy. Envy has been called a "just vice," not because it has anything to do with the virtue of justice but because the unpleasant emotions associated with envy serve as their own automatic, built-in punishment. Some people brag about their vices, such as gluttony, lust, or perhaps wrath, considering themselves liberated hedonists or people who don't mince their words and who put their cards on the table. Few people brag about their envy, although some may well rationalize that they are not envious. Envy is petty and small. It is an uncomfortable, shameful vice.

Before we dip into some time-tested remedies to help put envy to rest, we should also clarify a common confusion between *envy* and *jealousy*. Strictly put, *envy* regards our sadness in reaction to *someone else's good*, while *jealousy* regards our sadness at the prospect of losing some *good of our own*. Jealousy is possessive and suspicious, like the jealous spouse or friend who fears that if his spouse or friends associate with others, his relationship with them will be lost.

Both envy and jealousy can clearly be vices, but our focus here will be on the capital vice and deadly sin of green-eyed, blue-souled envy.

Is a Hulking Green-Eyed Monster Hiding in Your Conscience?

There is one sense in which envy might be hard to root out from the recesses of our conscience. Envy is born of pride, and we may be too proud to admit that this petty, mean-spirited vice is lurking about within us. Yet we won't be able to fool ourselves for long, because of the discomfort that envy brings to the forefront of our awareness. Let's think about it. When we've heard of someone else's good fortune or positive achievement, be it something simple and material such as getting a raise at the office, or acquiring a new house or car, or being honored for something noble and spiritual such as a good work performed for one's community, has our reaction been to rejoice with that person or to be made uncomfortable — to feel somehow that his success implies some deficiency in us? We would do well to train ourselves to catch these feelings of sadness about another person's good as soon as they cross our minds and sadden our countenances.

We need to hunt out those envious daughters as well, reminding ourselves that Thomas said they unfold in a sequence and asking ourselves questions such as these:

- When I have heard of someone's success, have I set envy into action through *tale-bearing?* Have I gossiped to others, trying to highlight that person's faults, showing others that he is not really "all that"? Do I really believe this somehow makes me a more valuable person?

- Regarding *detraction*, in the same situation, have I been so brazen as to diminish that person's accomplishment to his face? Have I teased or joked about him in his presence or in the presence of others with a malicious intent? Have I underhandedly slighted a peer's accomplishment by damning it with faint praise—by speaking positively about it but in a way that diminishes its true importance? Will his sadness serve to make me happy?

- If my efforts at tale-bearing or detraction have hit their mark, have I felt *joy at the other's misfortune*? If so, is this a joy that a follower of Christ should relish?

- If my tale-bearing or detraction has been to no avail, has my failure to harm left me *grieving at another's prosperity*? If so, do I see now how envy is a "just vice," with its own built-in penalty?

- If this process has gone on in me, do I understand and admit that these thoughts, feelings, and actions fuel a sinful *hatred*? Do I recognize that hatred is opposed to the virtue of love of neighbor? Is this how Christ wants me to live? How then can I crush this hatred and grow in the love of charity?

Sacramental Strategies: No Room for Envy in the House of God

Having examined our conscience for envy and its family, we are in just the right position to retain these insights until we can reach the door of a confessional. Our very act of confessing this embarrassing sin strikes at the pride that can foster it, and through the sacrament of Reconciliation even mortal sins of envy can be forgiven, opening our hearts again to the graces that flow from charity.

Reconciliation, though, is not the only sacrament that Christ has given us to combat envy. Let's heed the words of St. Paul.

Through the sacrament of Baptism we become "one body in Christ" (Rom. 12:5). Through the action of the Holy Trinity we are made brothers and sisters in Christ within the great Communion of Saints. St. Paul tells us, "Rejoice with those who rejoice, weep with those who weep" (Rom. 12:15). When God has showered some goodness on any of His children, who are we to begrudge it and to be saddened by it? When we think back upon the great sacrament of Baptism that gave us the indelible mark and seal of a member of the Body of Christ, it should spur us to accept God's continuing grace to share in the joy of our brothers and sisters.

Watching Your Steps So Envy Can't Trip You Up

It is not particularly difficult to watch the outward steps of envy in action. We've seen how the daughters of envy unfold in a visible sequence of behaviors. If we are to defeat this vice, however, we need to train ourselves to catch it before it has taken its first visible step, while it begins to fester within our souls.

Here again we hark back to Climacus's inward procession of the development of evil passions, those steps or stages of *provocation, coupling, assent, captivation, struggle,* and *passion.* You may or may not find the need to go through all six steps in your mind. To simplify things a bit, it might help to boil things down to a first stage of the "proto-passion" or "first movement," that first hint of awareness that you have heard or seen of someone's success and you reflexively get a pang of pain or sadness, a second stage or series of steps in which your rational mind begins to grapple with the implications of this reaction, determining, finally, the third stage of whether you fully experience the passion and harbor the vice of envy, waiting to express it in your actions if the opportunity should arise. I suggest we might condense these three steps to a kind of internal three Rs—not reading, 'riting, and 'rithmetic, but *reaction, reflection,* and *resolution.*

Recalling old Deputy Fife once more, for any assailing thought and potential sinful passion, we will be very well advised to nip it in the bud. I'm using the simple word *reaction* to encompass that early bud, the "proto-passion," "first movement," or provocation—the almost reflexive or automatic bodily reaction that sets the ball rolling. For envy, that initial reaction is going to be a discomfort or displeasure when we first find out about another's success. We are going to feel this like a reflex, unless we have, through the grace of God, and through our own cooperative efforts, developed the kind of virtues that can decondition this kind of envious reflex and perhaps transform it into a knee-jerk reaction, so to speak, of joy and not sorrow at another's good.

If we are ever going to get there, though, we do have work to do at catching these feelings early in ourselves and recognizing them for what they are. I feel them myself at times, and ironically, perhaps akin to Evagrius's suggestion for beginners in the spiritual life to pit one evil thought against another, I may feel tempted to use *pride* not to enkindle, but to ward off envy. "Such feelings of envy are beneath me!" I might be tempted to say this to myself, but surely there are better methods, since pride, as we've seen and will see, is even more vicious than the capital vices! A very simple start, nonetheless, is simply to become attuned to identifying these initial reactions in ourselves. "Uh oh, here is this icky feeling inside me. Is envy sneaking up upon me?"

When these initial reactions that enkindle the passion of envy have come to our conscious awareness, it is time for the stage of *reflection.* Climacus called the initial process here *coupling,* wherein we start a conversation within ourselves regarding the reaction or provocation. Will we feed the reaction with our thoughts and words, or will we try to counter it and nip it in the bud?

Recall here Evagrius's book on *Talking Back* to the eight assailing thoughts. He did not specifically address envy in his compilation of effective scriptural passages, because envy was not on the ancient list. (You remember from part I that it was included a couple of centuries later by Gregory.)

Still, we can certainly do our own talking back to budding thoughts of envy. Are there scriptural verses you can think of that put envy in its place? If envy is a problem for you, you might keep your eyes peeled for such verses and build for yourself an arsenal of them, such as Romans 12:5 and 12:15, mentioned earlier, which remind us that we are one in Christ and called to rejoice with those who rejoice. We can also get the conversation going by our own reflections upon the nature of envy and the sadness it can bring both to us and to the targets of our envy, if we act upon it and let loose its daughters. (And while you are at it, please take another gander at Venerable Louis of Granada's quotation that opened this chapter.)

The last stage of *resolution* captures whether virtue or vice, charity or envy has won out in our hearts. Of course, even if, in one particular instance, envy has won the battle and we've felt sadness at another's good and possibly taken action to spoil that person's party, so to speak, we can still take note of the negative results and try to learn from our failure what we might do to put envy in its place the next time such thoughts arise in us.

If You Pray for Those You Envy, You're Not Envying Very Well

To pray for those we envy is to pour down rain on our envy parade. Envy is sadness at another's good, a sadness that some may come to relish as the next best thing to having what the envied person has. To thank God for the goodness He has bestowed on the envied person and to petition Him to keep that good coming is a pretty direct counterattack on envy and all its daughters.

We can start by considering the very first words of the prayer that Christ Himself taught us in Matthew 6 — namely, of course, "Our Father." He taught us to say *our*, not *my*, Father, to remind us that we are all children of God, bound together with Christ in the Communion of Saints. We ask Him as well to give *us*, not *me*, our daily bread. We pray that God will give us the good things we need and that He will give them to our neighbor as well. The Our Father reminds us that God provides plenty of goodness to go around, and not just in terms of bread and other material goods. God helps us obtain all sorts of spiritual goods as well, and in the spiritual realm, the situation could not be further from a zero-sum game. One person's gain is not another person's loss. When any member of the Body of Christ grows in grace or virtue, we all should rejoice and share in the bounty.

If the vice of envy has turned us green or blue, we would be well advised to say the Lord's Prayer frequently with special emphasis on those words and ideas. We might also pray for the strength to recognize and eradicate envy within our souls and, any time we do recognize it, to name specifically in our petitions the person whom we have envied.

The Kinds of Virtues That Don't Take Kindly to Envy

Our prayers to conquer envy should remind us of our goal to build the virtues that will counter it in our thoughts, words, and deeds. We should pray for those virtues as well. *Kindness*, for instance, is an affectionate warmth and considerateness that expresses care for the welfare of others. It does not feel sad when another achieves something good; rather, it figures out how to help that person get it! As Fr. Lovasik notes in his masterful treatise on kindness,[55] Christ instructs us to *do* unto others as we would have them do unto us, not just to *react* to them. This means we are to be proactive. We're not to sit back and wait until they ask, but to think of active ways we can help and serve our neighbors, in ways that we would appreciate if we were in their position. Kindness mixes with envy no better than prayer does, although kindness and prayer go together very well. If envy has you in its vice grips, consider ending all of your prayers with the simple petition, "Lord, help me to be kind," and then get out there and be kind to every person you meet (even if, heaven forbid, some great goodness or honor may befall one of them!).

Another virtue foundational to the defeat of envy is *humility*, the word itself deriving from *humus* for earth, which is low and literally on the ground. When we are humble, we recognize our place in the hierarchy of God's universe. We don't decide who receives which particular gifts, talents, skills, virtues, achievements, or successes. That's up to God's providence. The humble will thank God for whatever He has given us without selfishly begrudging it when it appears as if He has given greater gifts to others. St. Paul tells us as much: "Do nothing from selfishness or conceit, but in humility count others better than yourselves" (Phil. 2:3).

[55] Lawrence G. Lovasik, *The Hidden Power of Kindness: A Practical Handbook for Souls Who Dare to Transform the World, One Deed at a Time* (Manchester, NH: Sophia Institute Press, 1999).

If we practice such humility, we will become less defensive, less wrapped up in concerns with our own self-esteem, and less envious. If we count others as better than ourselves, we will not feel the need to defend or parade our own inflated sense of self-importance. We will be less likely to suffer envy ourselves and less likely to be harmed by the envy of others toward us. An incident in the life of the ancient Stoic philosopher Epictetus expresses this nicely. When told that someone had talked about one of his faults (perhaps an act of *tale-bearing* produced by that person's *envy* of Epictetus), Epictetus showed no sadness or anger and did not try to defend himself. He merely responded (to paraphrase): "Surely he did not know about all my other faults, or he would have brought those up too!"

Incidents from the life of St. Martin de Porres ratchet up the virtue of humility even further. The son of a Spanish *hidalgo*[56] and a freed slave of African descent, the Dominican brother Martin was often taunted and called a "mulatto dog." Martin did not fight back, or merely shrug it off, but often sought these people out to do good works for them. When his friends reproved him for this, he would say, "These people truly know me." In the most poignant example, he was nursing an older ailing priest scheduled to have his leg amputated the next day. The priest started berating him and called him a mulatto dog, perhaps envying Martin's youth, his joy, or his health. A witness said Martin chuckled to himself as he left the room. He discerned that the priest had been craving a salad seasoned with capers.[57] He came

---

[56] Gentleman or noble.

[57] Edible flowerbuds used as seasoning. My wife had just made us a delicious salad with them a few days before I first came across this story!

back the next day and served the priest such a salad. The priest savored his meal and begged Brother Martin's forgiveness, and his leg was healed.

Humility then does not imply that we will rest content in mediocrity, or in our own failures or inactivity, but that we will strive to develop whatever talents we have been given, asking God's help to do so, while helping our neighbor to grow in God's grace too.

St. Thomas said that the vice of envy is contrary to the virtue of *charity*, and most specifically, to *the joy of charity at another's good*. When he explained the virtue of charity within the *Summa Theologica*, he stressed that charity is ultimately a form of *friendship with God*. We have been called into a loving, personal relationship with God, and God has commanded that our love for Him is also to be shown in loving our actions toward our neighbors. As Thomas so aptly sums it up: "The love of our neighbor requires that should we be not only our neighbor's well-wishers, but also his well-doers."[58]

Aristotle said we become builders by building and harpists by playing the harp. So too do we become lovers of our neighbors by loving our neighbors. If we put into daily practice little loving actions toward our neighbors, including loving actions toward those we might envy, we will become practiced, skillful, and joyful lovers. We might find too that we've gotten a little rusty at envy.

Immerse Yourself in the Communion of Saints

Do you feel sadness or joy when some great good comes to your child or your parent? Chances are that your immediate response

[58] *ST*, II-II, Q. 32. art. 5; cf. 1 John 3:18.

is one of great happiness and joy. We want good things for those we love, and their smiles become our smiles when good has come their way. Thomas compares the love of charity to the fires of a great furnace. Those closest to the furnace, our family and closest friends, naturally receive the most heat, but the more powerful the furnace of our love, the further will its warmth reach, even to strangers and enemies.

We should also recognize that the hotter the flames of our charity become, the more they will counter the dampening spirit of envy. As Catholic Christians, we must recall that we profess in the Creed our belief in the Communion of Saints. The saints in heaven and the would-be saints in purgatory and on earth are our children and our parents, our brothers and our sisters. As members of the Body of Christ, we *are* members of close family in which the good of any one should bring smiles of joy to any other.

As for the Church Triumphant in heaven, we can perhaps most easily heed St. Paul's admonition to think others better than ourselves. It is easy to acknowledge such spiritual superiority in the Church's great canon of saints. They stand so far above us in their holiness that most of us are not very likely to envy them. After all, when was the last time you felt saddened by St. Francis's compassion toward the poor, Blessed Mother Teresa's care for the sick, St. Maximilian Kolbe's self-sacrifice for a condemned man, or perhaps St. Thomas's towering and untiring theological achievements? We don't see them as competitors who threaten our self-esteem when our accomplishments are clearly so small in comparison.

We don't spend our time comparing ourselves with them. We should feel the same, though, toward all in the Church Militant. Every one of us on earth is called to be a saint. When we envy our neighbor's spiritual good, we might consider that we could well be envying a future saint.[59]

Even the Church Suffering in purgatory can help us in our battle against envy. When we pray for those souls that they may more quickly obtain that ultimate good of eternal union with God in heaven, we express joy at another's good, such compassionate joy in our hearts that will help ring the death knell for envy and its daughters.

Don't Envy Christ, Emulate Him

We are perhaps far less likely to envy the good of Christ Himself than that of any of His saints, and yet Jesus Christ Himself was indeed the target of envy throughout His life, from the envy of Herod in His infancy to the envy of the Scribes and Pharisees in the days leading up to His death. They felt that the spiritual good of Jesus diminished their own dignity and worth. They did not experience joy in His goodness, in His fulfillment of the promises of Scripture, but rather they unleashed envy and all its daughters, even the last and most wicked one of *hatred* that sought out Christ's death. So envy was a capital vice that contributed to Christ's placement on a cross.

So which of the seven last words that Christ uttered on the Cross did Fulton Sheen say counters the vice of envy? Luke tells

---

[59] Indeed, some great saints were envied greatly during their lifetimes on earth but thankfully were not dissuaded from their holy endeavors. Two examples that come first to mind are the attacks against the writings of St. Thomas Aquinas by some clerical academics of his day and some virulent modern attacks against the motives of Blessed Mother Teresa by some "new atheists" of our day.

that the rulers and the soldiers taunted Christ, saying that He saved others, but couldn't save Himself. The thief on the left chimed in and "railed at him saying, "Are you not the Christ? Save yourself and us!" (Luke 23:39). The thief on the right then rebuked the thief on the left, asking whether he did not fear God, since they had received the same condemnation, and yet although they were guilty, Christ was innocent. He asked Jesus to remember him when He got to his heavenly kingdom.

Sheen explains that the thief on the left envied Christ's goodness and power. He thought that if he himself had been given such power, he would have done things better, conquering all his enemies, rather than hanging from a cross. The thief on his right, though, realized his place in God's plan and that he was not and could not be the Savior. He was not saddened by Christ's goodness, but humbly asked to be allowed to share in it, and this Christ graciously and immediately granted him. This is when Christ uttered those last words contrary to envy: "Truly, I say to you, today you will be with me in Paradise" (Luke 23:43).

We would do well to meditate daily upon those words if we would put envy to rest. We were all made by God to seek Him and eventually to be one with Him in paradise. It is up to us whether we will accept His offer. We were made for joy, and so was our neighbor. We need to aid each other in living lives of grace and virtue, so that we may share in that joy together.

We should not envy Christ like the thief on the cross, but rather we should *emulate* Him. St. Thomas talked about emulation under the label of *zeal*, a zeal that prompts not sadness over another's good, not a desire that his good be removed from him, but a desire that we too might aspire to good by imitating the behavior of the person we strive to be like. It has been said that imitation is the highest form of flattery, and we are called to model ourselves after Christ. St. Paul could not have made it clearer: "Be imitators of me, as I am of Christ" (1 Cor. 11:1).

CHAPTER 10

Abolishing Avarice

'Tis the deepest of rest to wish for nought
beyond what due need calls for.

— **PRUDENTIUS**, *PSYCHOMACHIA*, V. 609[60]

It is not the man who has little who is poor,
but the one who hankers after more.

— **LUCIUS ANNEAUS SENECA**, *LETTER* II[61]

---

[60] "The Fight for Mansoul," in *Prudentius*, vol. 1, trans.
H. J. Thompson (Cambridge, MA: Harvard University
Press, 2006), 321.

[61] Seneca, *Letters from a Stoic* (New York: Penguin Books,
1969), 34.

Are You Possessed with Possessing?

We saw in part I that greed is not good, but then why do our souls seem restless, always hankering after more? Do we keep serving mammon? Perhaps we are possessed with possessing because of some virtue we lack. St. Thomas addressed the vice of *avarice* in his treatment of the cardinal virtue of *justice* and the specific virtue of *liberality*. Let's dip into the ways we can arm ourselves with these virtues then so when avarice tries to pull us down off our spiritual ladder, we can tell it where to go and knock it down a notch.

Examining Your Conscience for Too Many Dollar Signs

Would examining your conscience bear too striking a resemblance to examining your bank accounts or maybe your 401K? Money is not evil, but *the love of money* is.[62] Avarice, Thomas said, is "immoderate love of possessing." This means not a love of money in the sense that we will seek enough to meet our true needs, but in a sense that we feel we can never get enough. Does this hit us where we live? How much time do we devote to

---

[62] "For the love of money is the root of all evils; it is through this craving that some have wandered away from the faith and pierced their hearts with many pangs" (1 Tim. 6:10).

striving to obtain more money, to getting a better paying job, to stacking on overtime hours or part-time jobs, or perhaps delaying retirement to allow the pot to grow ever bigger?

These money-seeking behaviors may well be within reason, but we need to stop from time to time to ask ourselves if they really are. Will many of us look back at life in our last years and wish we had spent more time at the office or more time with our family and friends? When we search our conscience for signs of avarice, we might find that the fool's gold of riches has diverted us from the true gold of happiness that we obtain by serving God rather than mammon.

Let's run a little self-check of our spiritual account to see if we find any traces in the ledger of avarice's seven insatiable daughters:

- Have I employed *treachery, fraud, falsehood, perjury,* or *violence* to obtain greater riches? (If not, bravo! Five of the daughters are down for the count! Still, it's no time to raise our arm in victory or to reach it around and pat ourselves on the back. Many of us harbor avarice in our hearts without such bold attacks on the virtue of justice by taking from others what is rightfully theirs. Our avarice more likely smacks of *illiberality,* of a stinginess in freely sharing what does belong to us. So let's ask some questions to root it out.)

- Do I suffer *restlessness?* Not the kind of wandering of the mind that may come from the vice of sloth, in which I move from one thing to another because of a lack of spiritual joy, but the restlessness that comes from never being satisfied and always wanting to possess more, thinking of ways to get more and putting them into action? Am I a workaholic? Do I need to remind myself that while the vice of avarice is always restless and never satisfied, the virtues of hope and charity find their rest in God?

• Am I *insensitive to mercy*? Do I give freely, or am I what those in even Aristotle's day might call a skinflint or tightfisted? Am I generous in giving to charities and to the Church? Do I need to unclench my grip or to "let the wallet breathe" in a way that might provide some fresh air to others in need?

Eucharistic Gratitude Trumps Common Covetousness

When we have examined our conscience to determine to what extent we have let the love of money become the root of our personal evils, it is time to tell Christ, through the priest in the sacrament of Reconciliation.

And speaking of Christ and the sacraments, the greatest of all sacraments can also help us put an end to the vice of avarice. Christ Himself is present in the Eucharist, and it is only He who can give us the rest that money never can. "Come to me, all who labor and are heavy laden, and I will give you rest" (Matt. 11:28), He said to the crowd gathered around Him. Every time we gather around Him in the Sacrifice of the Mass, He is there to give us rest as well. Christ said, "My yoke is easy, and my burden is light" (Matt. 11:30). Christ's yoke is the yoke of charity, which works not to possess means to mere material goods, but so that we may rest with Christ. If avarice is a vice that weighs on your soul, then every time you receive Communion, think about resting in Christ, rather than restlessly laying up earthly treasures.

Watching the Steps of Avarice
All the Way to the Bank

For some of us, first stirrings of avarice will present themselves every day, so we need to be ready to respond to that first *reaction* of whatever begins to trigger avarice within our souls. We need to train ourselves then to nip them in the bud, perhaps first by calming ourselves whenever we find ourselves thinking of ways to make more money or perhaps to acquire more things that we don't really need. Does our restlessness reflect that we are not resting in God?

As we *reflect* on these thoughts, we'd do well to reflect on the many warnings in Scripture about giving money more than its rightful due. For example, we need to ask ourselves if we are feeding the root of all evils, serving mammon, making it hard to pass the gate into heaven, or laying up treasures on earth but not in heaven?[63]

How then will we *respond*? If avarice has wormed its way into our soul, we need to be able to give it away, which brings us to our next section.

Giving Greed Away

Our most direct counter to greed is simply to give it away. The "it" here refers not to the vice of avarice itself, of course. We surely don't want to pass that on to our neighbor, especially since he too may already be hoarding far more than his fair share of it! What we need to give away is that which avarice desires — immoderate possessions and riches. If we realize that we have been blessed with wealth and possessions far beyond what is needed to meet

---

[63] Cf. 1 Tim. 6:10; Matt. 6:19, 26; 19:24.

our actual needs, we will help quash avarice within our souls if we cultivate the virtue of generous giving, what St. Thomas calls *liberality*, freely giving, deriving from the Latin adjective *liber* for "free."

Thomas notes that the virtue of liberality is related to justice, since it involves our dealings with others involving external goods, but "justice gives another what is his, whereas liberality gives another what is one's own."[64] Further, justice considers "the legal due," while liberality "considers a certain moral due."[65] Liberality then is related to justice but is, in a sense, a generosity beyond the call of legal duty and of nature. As Thomas puts it so well, "to spend money on oneself is an inclination of nature; hence to spend money on others belongs properly to virtue."[66]

We must note as well that liberality does not imply recklessness in our giving. Thomas uses an apt military metaphor here, noting that a virtuous soldier's fortitude consists not only in wielding his sword in battle, but in sharpening it in between battles and storing it in its sheath. So too liberality means not only giving away money, but always using reasonable means to earn money and save it, so that it can be employed when it is truly needed. And speaking of fortitude, it has a related virtue of *magnificence*, deriving from *magnus* ("great") and *facere* ("to make or do").

The virtue of magnificence requires a willingness to suffer damage to one's pocketbook in order that great things can be made or accomplished. Think, for example, of the great cathedrals and basilicas throughout the ages, the multitude of Catholic

[64] *ST*, II-II, Q. 117, art. 5.
[65] Ibid.
[66] Ibid.

abbeys, missions, schools, and hospitals that have uplifted, educated, succored, and healed the world throughout the centuries, all funded by the magnificent liberality of countless donors. What a magnificent virtue is magnificence! How its aim at greatness squashes the pettiness of miserly avarice! How it unclenches the fingers of tightfistedness with its openhanded largesse!

Such a virtue of giving is not only for the rich. Virtues of liberality and magnificence are proportionate to our means. "Liberality," says Thomas, "depends not on the quantity given, but on the heart of the giver."[67] We need only remember the widow and her mite. The two small copper coins that she gave, worth about a penny, were valued more by Christ than the riches from the multitude, since she had "put in everything she had, her whole living" (Mark 12:41–44; Luke 21:1–4).

So how can we defeat avarice through the cultivation of liberality in our daily lives? Thomas reminds us that we must also employ the virtue of *prudence*, or practical wisdom, so that we give wisely. He notes that our money can be used in two main ways, either for our use or for the use of others. The first he calls *costs* or *expenditure*, and the second he calls *gifts*. Therefore, to thwart the illiberality of avarice and to build the virtue of liberality, we will act prudently in both the ways that we *spend* money on ourselves and in the ways that we *give* to others.

So how do we cultivate within ourselves the ability to act prudently with our money, guided by Christian charity? Here's one small suggestion: the next time you are tempted to buy some small thing you really don't need, maybe something as simple as a fancy coffee drink or a special desert, consider forgoing the treat, but adding the amount to your next donation

---

[67] *ST*, II-II, Q. 117, art. 2.

to a church, a worthy charity, or a person you know who is truly in need.

Immersing Yourself in the Things That Money Can't Buy

The vice of avarice and all its death-dealing daughters are spawned by too much focus on the material world. Of course, virtually every time we flip on our televisions, radios, computers, or phones we are bombarded with sights and sounds through endless enticing advertisements designed to keep our focus right there. It is no easy thing to avoid. You can't just hop in your car and drive away from it; the billboards will see to that. But we can train ourselves in how we think about all these lures toward materialism and consumerism and about whether we will let them foster within us the love of money and all the things it can buy. We can train ourselves to tone down the messages, to lessen our exposure to them, to turn off the car radio, the computer, the TV, or the phone for a while, to think and pray instead.

We can turn our mind toward higher things, such as the virtues that free us from vice, and to the lives and inspiration of those we know personally, and to the lives of the great saints, who have done magnificent things by putting the things of the spirit far above the things of the world. For example, the next time you find yourself plotting ways to stockpile more money than you really need, to buy more new things, to update last year's outdated electronic gadget, think of a magnificent and bounteous legacy that was left to all of us, when a man like St. Francis renounced avarice for things of the world and embraced Lady Poverty. To read the life of and strive to imitate any great saint and to pray for that saint's intercession is to work to open the tight fist of avarice that works to squeeze, constrict, and darken our hearts.

THE SEVEN DEADLY SINS

The Dollar Sign Meets the Sign of the Cross

Christ did not teach that money itself is evil, but rather the inordinate love of money that elevates it above its true importance and treats it as an end rather than as a means. He worked as a carpenter before His ministry began, and even during His ministry He paid Caesar what was Caesar's and instructed us to do the same (Mark 12:17). He personally embraced poverty, from His birth to a poor virgin in a stable, to the selection of His apostles. Wealth did not impress Him because things of the spirit are so much more impressive. He noted that the poor and those who are poor in spirit are blessed (Luke 6:20; Matt. 5:3). Avarice is not only for the rich. The poor, if they are not also poor in spirit, can also be covetous and miserly with the meager goods and wealth they have or seek to acquire. And the rich are not necessarily avaricious, if they use their wealth for the proper means and do not love it inordinately, insatiably seeking more. As Venerable Louis of Granada points out:

> As the poor by their poverty conform themselves to Jesus Christ, so the rich by their alms can conform their hearts to the merciful Heart of the Divine Model, who in his lowly crib received not only the shepherds with their simple tokens of affection, but also the wise and powerful men of the East, who came to lay at His feet the treasures of their gold and frankincense and myrrh.[68]

And as for the other end of Christ's life, as we move from the crib to the Cross, which of Christ's seven last words did Fulton J. Sheen see as a remedy for avarice? "Father, into thy hands I

---

[68] Louis of Granada, *The Sinner's Guide*, 277.

commit my spirit!" (Luke 23:46). Sheen tells us these words should teach us two lessons:

1. The more ties we have to the earth, the harder will it be for us to die.

2. We were never meant to be perfectly satisfied here below.[69]

These were the very last words that Christ uttered before His death, and we are well advised to heed their lessons for us. We've all heard the saying "You can't take it with you," and this has always been true of material things, as much as the richest of the rich from the time of the pharaohs have tried unsuccessfully to do so. All that any of us will have to take back to God on our own last day will be things of the spirit—of course, our very souls. If we remain entangled in avarice, it will serve to weigh us down, as Dickens's Jacob Marley wore shackles made heavy by his coveted money boxes. And not only will avarice make it harder for us to go to heaven; it will make it harder for us to face the fact that someday our spirits will depart from earth. There will be no more dollars to earn, no more goods to accumulate, and we will be judged by the weight not of our wealth, but of our charity.

The second lesson harkens back to our opening quotations for this chapter. Prudentius knew that we will achieve complete rest, desiring nothing at all inordinately, only when we achieve the beatitude of union with God in heaven. Seneca, himself a very rich man, but with a noble spirit, knew that no amount of earthly riches would ever completely satisfy him, or for that matter, anyone else.

[69] Sheen, *The Seven Capital Sins*, 87.

Let's conclude our treatment of avarice with three brief anecdotes from the life of St. Thomas that also end with the Cross of Christ. One story holds that when Thomas and some friars approached the great city of Paris, a brother friar stated how grand it would be to own all of that city's vast wealth. St. Thomas replied that he would rather have a copy of St. John Chrysostom's *Homilies on the Gospel of St. Matthew*! Another story tells of a rich man who conversed with St. Thomas through the streets of Paris and insisted that Thomas allow him to buy him a generous gift. St. Thomas requested that he buy him all the caged birds being sold on the street so that he could set them free! Finally, St. Thomas once had a vision of Christ. Christ told him he had written well and asked Thomas what He could give him. Thomas replied, "Only you, Lord."

CHAPTER 11

Vanquishing Vainglory

Vainglory is the glory that we give ourselves; either for what is not really in us, or for what is in fact in us but not owing to anything we did, or for what is in us and owing to us but which does not deserve to be the cause of a boast....

There are those who are proud and haughty because they ride a magnificent horse or because their hat sports a fancy feather, or because they are wearing some fashionable clothing. Who does not see the folly here? If there is glory due, it belongs to the horse, the bird or the tailor! And what a pitiable heart is his who expects esteem because of a horse, a feather or some lace!

—ST. FRANCIS DE SALES,
INTRODUCTION TO THE DEVOUT LIFE[70]

[70] St. Francis de Sales, *Introduction to the Devout Life: A Popular Abridgment*, abridged by Madame Yvonne Stephan (Rockford, IL: TAN Books, 1990), pt. III, chap. 5, 126.

Are You Seeking Glory in All the Wrong Ways?

Our next deadly vice, vainglory, bears close family ties to the deadly vice of envy. Sometimes we envy the honor and glory that others receive because we are frustrated that we do not have it. The more vainglorious we are, the more likely we are to feel envious when others sing the praises of someone besides us! Still, we are to strive to do things worthy of praise to glorify God through our actions. What then is the glory we seek in vain? Let's seek a little wisdom first from the Angelic Doctor.

According to St. Thomas, there are three ways glory can be vain, and these can be seen on the part of the following:

1. The *things* which for which one seeks glory are vain or petty.

2. The *persons* from whom one seeks glory are uncertain and lacking in judgment.

3. The *end* for which glory is sought is not to magnify God's honor or to help the spiritual welfare of one's neighbor, but to glorify oneself.[71]

In a nutshell then, the glory we seek is vain if we seek glory for the *wrong things*, from the *wrong people*, or for the *wrong reasons*.

---

[71] *ST*, II-II, Q. 132, art. 1.

Moving from the seed to the full-grown weed of vainglory, we can add St. Francis de Sales's insights from the quotation at the start of this chapter that we also see vainglory in action when we seek glory for *deeds we didn't really do*, or *virtues we don't really have*, for good things or characteristics we do have *but did not earn*, or for goods that we have that "*do not deserve to be the cause of a boast*" (the vain or petty things in St. Thomas's point 1).

Having examined the nature of this vainglorious enemy of spiritual growth, let's move right along to form some effective battle plans.

Mirror, Mirror on the Wall, Who's the Vainest of Them All?

How fitting that when we gaze at our face in the mirror in the morning, we most likely do so from behind a cabinet known as a *vanity*! Although those of us who spend too much time there may well be guilty of vanity, of caring a bit too much about how we appear to others, we do need to give *our souls* a long, hard look in the mirror every day, if we are to root out vainglory. When we stand in front of that mirror, whether real or metaphorical, we'd do well to ask ourselves a series of questions, if we'd like to obtain our true spiritual reflection:

- Do I seek notice and praise from others, or even try to instill their envy, for temporal, passing things such as the kind of car I drive, the clothes or jewelry I wear, or perhaps the names that I drop?

- Do I strut and seek honor for positive traits that are not of my doing? Do I figuratively (and literally) look down on others because of my great physical height? What did I do to achieve that? "Who can add to his stature by

138

one cubit?" (cf. Matt. 6:27). Do I feel better than others and more worthy of praise because of my good looks or perhaps because of the wealth or accomplishment of my parents or ancestors? If any glory is due, shouldn't it truly go to the God, who gave these good things to me, so that I could do good things for His glory?

And we must not forget to look for sins of vainglory's deadly daughters:

- Have I been vainglorious through my words by *boasting*? Do I really believe such self-aggrandizement raises me in the eyes of others? Do I admire most those who center all conversation on themselves or those who show genuine interest by asking about the affairs and deeds of others?

- Have I sought to show my intellectual excellence and superiority over others through *obstinacy*, through failing to yield to another a point that was well made but contrary to mine?

- Am I an "aginner" like those in the old country saying who, regardless of what others are "fer," are outspoken "agin' it"? In other words, have I been courting vainglory's daughter of *discord*? Have I been unwilling to concede to others in matters contrary to what I will, even if deep down, I know I have been wrong?

- Have I been *contentious*, quarreling with others, unwilling to admit that I could be wrong or that my own will need not always prevail? Do I always have to have or do it my way?

- Have I been *disobedient?* Have I disobeyed directives from my boss, office administrators, or perhaps disregarded traffic, tax, canon, or civil laws, because I believe I always know better?

Confession and Confirmation Can Vanquish the Vice Vainglory

Having taken a good look in the spiritual mirror, we are in the best position to confess our sins of vainglory, so that God may absolve them and we may resolve to fight them more ardently from here on out.

Another sacrament we'd do well to avail ourselves of in the fight against vainglory is that of our Confirmation. Thomas said that we are brought to our bishop for Confirmation, "as to the commander of an army."[72] By Baptism we become members of Christ, and by Confirmation we become "Christian soldiers." Here we receive through the bishop's ministrations the special inflowing of the seven gifts of the Holy Spirit, the gifts of wisdom, understanding, counsel, fortitude, knowledge, piety, and fear of the Lord.[73] These gifts give us strength and the weapons to fight the good fight of the spiritual life. They draw our minds toward the higher things of God and give us the strength to pursue them. Those who willingly accept those seven graces from God and put them into practice in their lives will not have much time to worry about what others might think of their car or their horse or their hat or their shoes or their gargantuan TV screen or their skill at some game or whatever the vainglorious case may be.

[72] *ST*, III, Q. 71, art. 10.
[73] Cf. Isa. 11:1–2.

Watching the Steps of Vainglory from the Perch of an Outside Observer

Harking back to our condensation of Climacus's six steps toward vice into the three steps of *reaction*, *reflection*, and *response*, if vainglory is our bane, we need to learn to catch ourselves early.

As for the *reaction* phase of the first stirrings of vainglory, when we see an item we'd like to buy, we need to ask ourselves from the start if it is something we really need or something we think will impress others. When we have the urge to talk to someone about a recent accomplishment, we need to ask ourselves whether there's some question we can ask the other person about what's up in his life. Have we started to daydream about honor and praise from others? If so, we need to wake ourselves fast!

When *reflecting* on vainglorious impulses, we might want to consider as well how our vainglorious acts may truly appear to others, often leading them not to respect us, but to dislike or to pity us. When we unleash those daughters of *boasting*, *obstinacy*, *contention*, *discord*, and *disobedience*, people will be less likely to detect in us some excellence and more likely to sense our inferiority parading as superiority. We need to ask ourselves if we are seeking glory for the wrong things, with the wrong people, and for the wrong reasons, and talk back to ourselves if we are.

As for the outcome of our *response* to vainglorious impulses, if we have succumbed and acted upon them, we need to observe carefully any negative consequences in the reactions of others and within our own souls, so we may be encouraged to make amends to others and to battle all the harder next time.

Prayer Puts True Glory Right Where It Belongs

What more appropriate prayer to counter our selfish vainglory than the Glory Be? "Glory be to the Father, and to the Son, and to the Holy Spirit, as it was in the beginning, is now, and ever shall be, world without end. Amen." This prayer places glory where it belongs and should remind us that any glory we seek should be not for vain things but for truly meritorious deeds that will give glory to God and inspire others to do so as well. If vainglory is your bane, why not draw up a simple battle plan to pray the Glory Be slowly and thoughtfully, literally "morning, noon, and night"—before or just after getting out of bed, during the lunch hour, and just before going to sleep?

Fortitude Conquers Most Difficult Vices

Recall that St. Thomas addresses vainglory within his treatise on the virtue of *fortitude*. Fortitude is that virtue of the irascible appetite that enables us to obtain the "arduous," or difficult, goods by doing battle with things that keep us from those goods. An allied virtue is that great-souledness of *magnanimity*, which seeks out truly great things and does not bother with trifles.

So how is vainglory contrary to fortitude and magnanimity? Well, we have seen that vainglory can entail vigorous efforts to obtain things *that are not truly good*. If we employ the virtues of fortitude and magnanimity, and indeed, the Holy Spirit's gift of fortitude as well, we will have the courage to seek out worthy and difficult achievements even when they are not glorious in the eyes of the world. Many who would seek spiritual goods may be ridiculed and scorned by others who seek glory for themselves through things that the world sees as good. Virtually our entire modern advertising and entertainment industries prompt us to try to obtain happiness through material things and through fame for hollow deeds. Let's ask ourselves how we can work up our ire against the fact that we so often let them lead us by the nose. Let's use our noses instead to smell that rat of vainglory and fortify our spirits to chase it from our souls.

Immersing Oneself in the True, the Good, and the Beautiful

If we can train ourselves see the true, the good, and the beautiful things of the world for what they truly are — partial, imperfect reflections of the totality of Truth, Beauty, and Goodness of God in all His glory, then will we see vainglory for what it truly is — the false, the evil, and the ugly. Then every time we feel tempted to brag or strut or in some other way draw attention to ourselves, we'll remember how vain and how paltry such pseudo-glory is.

Burying Vainglory beneath the Cross of Christ

If we wish to keep our eyes focused on higher and truly most glorious things, from time to time they will rest upon the figure on the Cross. Which of Christ's last seven words on the Cross did Fulton Sheen apply to the sin of vainglory? Well, the good archbishop used the roster of seven deadly sins that lists *pride* instead of vainglory. This poses no problem for us, though, since even Gregory and Thomas acknowledge the close linkage and how vainglory proceeds so directly from pride. Now, here are the words of Christ: "My God, my God, why hast thou forsaken me?" (Matt. 27:46; Mark 15:34).

Sheen notes that these words of desperation before His death reveal Christ's ultimate rejection of pride and vainglory. Recall those who are vainglorious about their ancestry and pedigree. Christ's pedigree, so to speak, included King David on earth and God the Father in heaven, yet He sought quite the opposite of vain glories for himself on earth. Rather, He made Himself the lowest of the low during His time on earth so that all true glory would go to his heavenly Father. When Christ came to earth, he displayed the ultimate act of humility, recalling that the very word *humility* refers to the earth. With Christ on the Cross as our model, we would do well to imagine that we have buried our pretensions to vainglory deep in the ground underneath Christ's Cross.

CHAPTER 12

Gutting Gluttony

On the contrary, Gregory says (*Moral*. xxx, 18) that
unless we first tame the enemy dwelling within
us, namely, our gluttonous appetite, we have not
even stood up to engage in the spiritual combat.

— *SUMMA THEOLOGICA*, II-II, Q. 148, ART. 1

Are You Too Stuffed to Enter into the Spiritual Fray?

As our spiritual combat moves on to the fifth of the seven capital vices, we need to make sure we are standing at the frontlines of battle and not just sitting on the sidelines, feeding that gluttonous enemy within us. Gluttony is the first of the bodily, carnal sins for which we'll prepare to do battle.

How odd that eating disorders of various sorts, from the relatively rare mental impairments of anorexia nervosa and bulimia to the veritable epidemic of adulthood and childhood obesity, are so well known and such hot topics of conversation, while the ancient vice of gluttony is rarely a topic of discussion, even in our churches. Just think, when was the last time you heard a homily on gluttony? In fact, I'd wager a half-pound bar of chocolate that you've heard more invitations to donuts after Mass in the parish hall than you've heard homilies on gluttony. This is not to say that donuts (let alone chocolate) cannot be very good things, but it does seem we've lost the ancient awareness that when we forsake reason when it comes to eating, we are likely to forsake it in many more areas of our physical and spiritual lives as well. As the philosopher Seneca once stated, "He will have many masters who makes his body his master." We need to find out then how to fight the vice of gluttony and its daughters so that they will not master us and pull us from the many fronts on which we must wage our many spiritual battles. Let's cinch up our belts and get to it.

Examining the Conscience
for the Enemy Dwelling within Us

Not every person who is over the average body weight for his height is necessarily suffering from the vice of gluttony, and not every person who is as lean as can be and as fit as a fiddle is necessarily free of gluttony. God has graced us all with our unique body types. Just take a look around, and you'll see that we come in all shapes and sizes. A twentieth-century American psychologist, William Herndon Sheldon, popularized the classification of three basic body types or "somatotypes" (deriving from the Greek *soma* for "body") as the thin-boned *ectomorphs* tending toward leanness and lankiness, the thick-boned *mesomorphs* tending toward muscularity, and the medium-boned *endomorphs* tending toward development of fat. These tendencies reflect the unique individual genetics we receive from our parents, and we can all be graded on a scale as to what extent we show characteristics of each type. People of all somatotypes can be fit and healthy, and the presence or absence of the vice of gluttony cannot necessarily be found by determining whether a person is skinny, fat, or muscular. Gluttony is more than skin deep. As Gregory noted, it is an enemy that dwells deep within us!

Gluttony is *an inordinate, unreasonable desire for food and drink.* We can begin to pinpoint it in ourselves by asking ourselves if we manifest what St. Thomas called gluttony's "species." So, just ask yourself questions like these:

- Do I simply eat *too much*? Have I noticed my weight increasing, my belt feeling tighter? Am I experiencing stomachaches, reflux, or fitful sleep by eating too much before sleep? If so, can I shrink down those portions?

- Do I eat too *greedily*? Do I wolf down my food? If so, can I strive to slow myself down by setting my utensils down between bites to have a sip of water, or to share a word with my family?

- Do I eat too *hastily*? Do I have a hard time waiting for the dinner bell? Am I able to keep the brief fasts between planned meals and planned snacks? If not, can I strive to do so, to wait a bit when hunger pangs appear, to do something else and hold off until the next meal? Can I consider offering up the minor discomfort?

- Do I eat too *sumptuously* or too *daintily*? Do I expect only fine foods at every meal, prepared to my particular liking? If so, can I come to appreciate and thank God for the vast array of simple, healthy, tasty foods He has provided?

These species of gluttony share the common denominator of giving food more than its rightful due, of thinking about it too much, of overvaluing it to the point at which we may harm the health of our bodily temple or disrupt the shared communal experience of a meal through our poor table manners. Recalling Gregory's words, if we haven't mastered our gluttony, the "enemy within" that ravages our body, we're not in a very good position to build a spiritual life. Excessive desire for food takes our mind off higher things, excessive consumption makes us lethargic and bloated, rendering us less capable of charitable actions, and seeking excess comfort for our bellies makes us less apt to imitate Christ through suffering and sacrifice. If we are

THE SEVEN DEADLY SINS

experiencing these spiritual effects of gluttony, then it is time to examine our conscience for gluttony's daughters too:

- When overstuffed with food or intoxicated with too much drink have I let loose any of gluttony's daughters of *unseemly joy, scurrility, uncleanness, loquaciousness,* or *dullness of mind as regarding understanding?*

- Have I felt *unseemly joy* about such excess with little thought of the damage to my body or of the possible harm to others who depend on my being in good health or even those who may happen to share the same road home?

- Has my overeating or drinking led me to *loquaciousness,* to hurtful words or poorly judged jests?

- Have I acted the fool in such states of excess, committing acts of buffoonery or *scurrility* that might offend others and might seem foolish to me in a more sober state?

- Has my gluttony or drunkenness led to *uncleanness* in body or mind?

- Have I let food or drink cloud my ability to think clearly and reason, *dulling my understanding* through lethargy or intoxication?

Fessing Up Our Gluttony

The grace of the sacrament of Reconciliation can absolve the taint of any of the seven deadly sins, including gluttony. I'll wager, though, that just as few homilies focus on gluttony, so too do few confessions! After all, when was the last time you confessed to the priest that you supersized your fries? We know from our Thomistic analysis of gluttony, though, that this capital vice entails far more than eating too many oily, salty potatoes, because true gluttony has serious spiritual consequences. It is another way that we can be distracted from the things of God and the needs of our neighbor by focusing excessively on selfish bodily pleasures. Serious sins of gluttony truly can and should be included in one's confession when they are ferreted out in one's examination of conscience.

Of course, the ultimate sacrament can also come to our aid in the battle against gluttony; indeed, it even has a small fast built right in! Fasting has been associated with the liturgy since the days of the apostles (Acts 13:2), and prior to 1964 the Eucharistic fast began at midnight. Now, barring exceptions for those such as the elderly and the sick and their caretakers, we are to fast at least one hour before receiving the Eucharist. This fast prepares us physically and spiritually to receive the true Bread of Life. It is a penance for our sins and an act of temperance that mortifies bodily desires in preparation for the reception of Christ. It should build in us a hunger and thirst for Christ. So then it would behoove us to reflect on the fact that we already practice a brief fast on regularly and to look for other opportunities to abstain from food purposely or to eat smaller portions or fewer meals to grow in our life in Christ.

It's Easy to Watch Our Steps toward Gluttony

It is easy to watch the steps toward gluttony when those steps lead to the refrigerator or perhaps to our office's vending machine. But our feet would not be stepping in that direction unless some previous steps had been taken within our mind. One of the best ways to stop those mental steps in their tracks is to try to minimize our initial reaction to gluttonous thoughts by avoiding the occasion of incitements to such thoughts, such as the sights and smells of foods at times when we don't need to eat. This is not easily done, since anyone who watches television is bombarded by food commercials and one driving down the street is bombarded by billboards with giant cheeseburgers and the like.

Still, we do have opportunities to exert some control over our stimulation toward gluttony, especially within our own homes. This can include techniques such as leaving no tempting foods out on the counter, but tucking them all into the cupboards, and leaving no food on the table after filling our plate at mealtimes, so as to avoid the temptation to have a second (or third) helping. These are clear, straightforward examples of avoiding the near occasions of incitements to the sin of gluttony. Simple techniques like these can help keep us from eating too much and too often.

We can also help curb our tendencies to eat too much, too often, or too quickly by planning some snacks within our daily routine between three modest meals. If we plan to have one or two or even three small treats of perhaps 100 to 200 calories in midmorning, in mid-afternoon, or after dinner, this can help keep from getting ravenously hungry between those three reasonable meals.

We can also counter any urges to eat sumptuously or daintily by exercising a little mortification and making sure that the majority of our snacks and meals comprise simple, everyday relatively unprocessed foods, from the basic food groups of dairy, grains, fruits, vegetables, and lean meats, while limiting specially prepared and prepackaged foods. In our modern grocery stores this usually means shopping from around the store's outer walls while being wary of what lies within! Those inner aisles usually lack refrigeration and are where most of the heavily processed foods lurk, many being foods that have been stripped of natural fiber and loaded with sugar, salt, and preservatives, so they taste great, are less filling, and fire up your appetite for more.

Another tip is to be leery of so-called light, lite, or diet foods; to create them, manufacturers suck out some of the calories, fats, or sugars of the regular versions of such foods, but these "watered down" (sometimes literally) versions of foods can be less satisfying and leave us eating more than we would have in the first place or leave us hungry enough to seek out something else too, whether "light," "lite," "diet," or not. By relying heavily on such foods and drinks, we act as if we would cure our foods, rather than ourselves, of gluttony!

So then, if hunger is stirred within us between meals, we will be best prepared to cope with it when we have also planned a healthy snack, so we never go too far between meals.

We might also reevaluate our meals to be sure we are not eating *too sparsely* to meet our bodily needs for nutrition, thus unwittingly triggering, through our good intentions, the gnawing need to gnaw needlessly between meals! We should ideally include a reasonable amount of protein and fat from meat, eggs, chicken, fish, milk, cheese, nuts, nut butters, or beans, along with some natural and complex carbohydrates from vegetables, fruits, or whole grains with each of our main meals. We should arise from the table satisfied, neither overly full nor still hungry.

If the hunger pangs still hit, another effective bodily technique is to have on hand a large glass of ice water. The water helps fill the stomach and is good for hydration and overall health. Plus, the body has to expend energy to heat the cold water to our internal body temperature of 98.6 degrees. So, by drinking water instead of eating food you don't need, you are not only avoiding extra calories, but you're also burning a few.

If gluttony should get the best of us and we find we have eaten too much, too soon, too ravenously, or too daintily, we will also have the chance to put ourselves back on track by practicing dietary temperance in our very next meal by eating more reasonable smaller portions, not eating before mealtime, slowing down our pace, and eating simple, wholesome foods, giving thanks to God all the while.

Prayer Deflates Gluttony

Fasting and prayer have long gone together, since when we mortify our bodies we can become more attuned to sanctifying our souls. If you are tempted to eat before a meal, consider the option of praying instead, and by all means include petitions for the temperance to conquer gluttony.

Still, eating and prayer can be perfect partners too. We know this through our familiar prayers before meals: "Bless us, O Lord, and these Thy gifts which we are about to receive from Thy bounty, through Christ our Lord. Amen." Have we established the habit of saying this prayer before every meal of which we partake? And have we really paid attention to those words? If we truly recognize our food as a gift from God, will we be as likely to show ingratitude by asking for more than we are served? Will we insist that it is prepared exactly to our liking?

Also, have you established the habit of praying after meals? Here is a traditional Catholic prayer: "We give Thee thanks for all Thy benefits, O Almighty God, who livest and reignest world without end. Amen. May the souls of the faithful departed, through the mercy of God, rest in peace. Amen." This can reinforce the spirit of gratitude in our hearts, and by our praying for the faithful departed, the prayer transforms the simple act of eating into an opportunity to let our thoughts and prayers rise beyond ourselves. Of course, the Lord's Prayer too, can be a great aid in the battle against gluttony. We pray "give us this day our daily bread"—not two or three days' worth!

Temperance Guts Gluttony

The virtue of temperance in regard to our desire for food and drink clearly shows how virtues aim at "golden means," avoiding deficiency and excess. If we are to conquer gluttony, we must acquire the temperance to avoid eating too much or too little, and indeed, to avoid even thinking too much or too little about the role of food in our daily lives. Some people who go on extreme diets, *eating* much *too little*, are the most likely to go to the other extreme in *thinking* far *too much* about food, metaphorically (or literally) salivating as they wait in anticipation of their next meal!

The virtue of temperance in regard to our desire for food and drink also clearly shows, as Aristotle and St. Thomas were always fond of pointing out, that virtues are essentially good habits. Vices, such as gluttony, are essentially bad habits. If we are to conquer the bad habit of gluttony, we must build the contrary virtue of dietary temperance. We become builders by building, harpists by playing the harp, and temperate eaters by eating temperately—ideally every day. This is the key to why most diets succeed in the short run and fail in the long run. Most people who go on a diet lose weight while they are on the diet and regain the weight when they go off the diet. The extreme measures of limited or unsavory food choices and their time-limited nature do not lead to the development of the virtue of dietary temperance that can be practiced throughout one's life on earth.

If our goal in controlling our gluttony is not a quick fix to look better in a swimsuit, but an attempt to tend to our bodily temples properly and to glorify God in the process, we need to strive every day to acquire the virtue of temperance as it applies to our daily food and drink. This entails learning about healthful eating and nutrition and then putting it into practice every day of our lives.

Time to Rise to the Spiritual Battle

God crafted every human as a beautiful unity of body and soul, of matter and spirit, both of which are good, very good. We are easily led astray, though, when we succumb to the urges of the body that would lead us away from the goods of the soul. In regards to the capital vice of gluttony, its several unsavory species, and its corps of corpulent daughters, we will be best prepared to do spiritual battle when we simply regain the ancient awareness that the seemingly old-fashioned, outdated, and all-but-forgotten sin of gluttony remains alive and well, more than happy to keep us sitting on the spiritual sidelines. If we recall the words of St. Gregory, we will strive to keep gluttony from removing us from the good fight for the things of the spirit.

No Time for Gluttony While Bearing the Cross

If we wish to win the battle against gluttony, we'd also do well to remember some of the last words of Christ. Archbishop Sheen declares that Christ's words "I thirst" (John 19:28) were spoken in reparation for the sins of gluttony. Here is Christ, who said, "If any one thirst, let him come to me to drink" (John 7:37), dying of thirst on the Cross, and He is given but a sponge dipped in vinegar.[74] Christ certainly experienced physical thirst, but He speaks to us of the spiritual thirst for love and for eternal life.

Christ recognized the value of food and drink for the perseveration of human life and for enjoyment. He willingly dined with others, indeed with those disdained by others, such as tax collectors and prostitutes. He sought to share material food with them while He opened their hearts to the spiritual food He would bring them. He multiplied loaves and fishes to feed thousands and to give them a foretaste of the way He would miraculously multiply His own Body and Blood as spiritual food for countless billions who would follow them. He fasted, not because food was bad, but because it was so good, and His example would show us that to abstain from food at times helps us tame and mortify our desires, so that our bodies become better controlled by our spirit.

So then, the next time we realize that the deadly vice of gluttony faces us on the field of spiritual battle, we should call to our aid Christ Himself, who chose to endure hunger and thirst so that He could provide us with real food and real drink that we can share within Him forever.

---

[74] In fulfillment of the prophecy of the psalmist: "For my thirst they gave me vinegar to drink" (Ps. 69:21).

CHAPTER 13

Leveling Lust

Do not imagine that you will overwhelm the demon of fornication by entering into an argument with him. Nature is on his side and he has the best of the argument. So the man who decides to struggle against his flesh and to overcome it by his own efforts is fighting in vain. The truth is that unless the Lord overturns the house of the flesh and builds the house of the soul, the man wishing to overcome it has watched and fasted for nothing. Offer up to the Lord the weakness of your nature. Admit your incapacity and, without your knowing it, you will win for yourself the gift of chastity.

—ST. JOHN CLIMACUS[75]

[75] St. John Climacus, *The Ladder of Divine Ascent*, 173.

Are You Ready to Admit That You Can't Conquer Lust on Your Own?

Next we encounter the second carnal capital vice of lust, that vehement desire for inordinate pleasures of the flesh. This sin threatens to hit us all where we live, since we all obtain life through the act of sexual union, and our powerful, species-preserving impulses toward sexual behaviors are under nearly constant assault from temptations to sins of lust in thoughts, desires, words, and deeds. To combat this powerful sin of the flesh will require far more than ordinary weapons. As St. John Climacus makes clear, we will have no chance of winning this battle if we plan to rely on our own strength. Rather, the first step we must take and never step away from is to admit that we cannot do it alone and to ask God to strengthen us with supernatural, spiritual weaponry.

Examining the Conscience for Corrupted Concupiscence

The most obvious, direct, and pernicious enticements to lust, such as those of Internet pornography, have grown exponentially in recent years, and many men (and women), even those with informed consciences who know the dangers, struggle against their lustful addictions. Perhaps the most deadly consequence of lust in our modern world is the mind-boggling number of abortions performed in this nation today. Sex itself has become a god like Moloch, with innocent babes plucked from their mothers' wombs for sacrifice upon its altar.

Still, even for those who would never consider seeking out pornographic materials or supporting abortion, our modern popular entertainment culture and media still surround us at every turn and threaten to engulf us in body and soul with blatant incitements to lust. They have become so highly sexualized for profit that our consciences may become numb, leaving us insensitive to the extent that we have become entangled within the countless tentacles of this deadly vice. We need to wake ourselves up and root out the lustful habits that may lurk within our souls with questions such as these:

- Do I thoughtlessly read modern books or watch modern movies that glamorize and glorify sinful sexual behaviors or listen to popular songs that promote illicit sexuality and besmirch the potential beauty and goodness of human sexuality?

- If so, do I tell myself that I ignore those bad parts and am not influenced by them? (That is not likely true, and even if it is, if I have paid money for such products, have I considered how I have helped the producers create more of such products potentially leading countless others toward sin?)

- Are there other ways that I put myself in the path of lustful thoughts and behaviors by the media I consume, the products I purchase, or the places I go?

- When I find myself entertaining lustful thoughts triggered by a person or an image I see or by a memory, do I enjoy and embellish the thought, or do I seek to dismiss it? Have I trained myself to see how such thoughts damage and dishonor the dignity of my state in life, whether single, married, widowed, or in the religious life?

- As for the precursors of lust, have I failed to fight the battles for self-control against gluttony or drunkenness that may fuel my tendencies toward lust?

- As for lust's eight daughters, have I searched my conscience for instances of *blindness of mind, thoughtlessness, inconstancy, rashness, self-love, hatred of God, love of this world,* and *abhorrence of a future world?* Even if I haven't committed fornication, adultery, or other blatant sexual sins, have I done so in my heart? Have I dishonored my spouse by giving excessive attention to others of the opposite sex? Have I dishonored my single or religious state by similar thoughts, if not deeds? Have I rationalized sexual sins, substituted my own judgment for God's? Have I *thanked* God for human sexuality, and shown gratitude and love for him by seeking to purify my thoughts?[76]

Sacramental Healing of Body and Soul

Having examined our conscience for potential sins of lustful thoughts, desires, words, and deeds, it is time to seek out the sacrament of Reconciliation. God's grace can forgive all manner of sexual sins if our repentance is genuine. We should remember

---

[76] "Blessed are the pure in heart, for they shall see God" (Matt. 5:8).

that sins of lust can be very embarrassing and shameful because in them we allow ourselves to operate at the animal level, guided by the pleasures of sensation, rather than the restraint of our human reason. This is no reason not to confess them, however. Through confessing these sins, we acknowledge our weakness and ask for God's strength. We should not worry much about shocking our priestly confessor either, for the priest is also a man, and throughout the history of the Church countless sinners have struggled with sexual sins and laid their hearts bare to Christ's ministers. In fact, in addition to absolution, we are likely to receive wise counsel in dealing with the particular desires or deeds of lust that are weighing on our soul.

Other sacraments can help us battle lust as well. We need to recall that through Baptism we have become members of the Body of Christ, and our bodies have become temples of the Holy Spirit, temples we must honor. Through Confirmation we have been made strong to fight the good fight against all manner of vices. If we are married, we need to recall and employ the grace that God has given us through the sacrament of Matrimony to employ our sexuality as befits our marital state, in loving self-giving to our spouse with openness to new life. Those who have received Holy Orders need to recall that special graces that God will give them to prevail in a celibate state, both in exterior acts and in interior thoughts.

How to Keep Lust from Doing the Quickstep

As we have analyzed the various steps through which the first inklings of a temptation toward sin may mature into full-blown sin itself, we have tended to emphasize that stage after the first initial *reaction*, the stage we have called *reflection* (most akin to Climacus's stage of *coupling*), in which we debate within our souls whether we will yield to the temptation and produce the *response* of sin. So powerful and quick-acting are the sensory stimuli (sights, sounds, smells) that lead to thoughts of lust that we might say that they do the quickstep, although theirs is a deadly dance.

Climacus tells us clearly that we are not going to overwhelm "the demon of fornication," by challenging him in an argument. Our reason alone is too limited. How many otherwise great wise men and women have been brought low through succumbing to the stirrings of lust without calling upon the grace of God? So, perhaps having just emerged from the sacrament of Confession, or having completed our prayers or devotional reading, we must not be overconfident that we will have the wherewithal to conquer the stirrings of lust the next time they knock on the door of our concupiscence. We need to trust in God, rather than in our rational powers alone.

So then, when we are first aware of the initial stirrings of lust, we had better immediately seek God's help, perhaps by a prayer that is very swift and powerful, such as the ancient Jesus Prayer that the Desert Fathers were so fond of: "Lord Jesus Christ, have mercy on me, a sinner." Hereby, we immediately call out for Christ's help to cast out the demon of fornication, even though the demon might lie within our own concupiscence. Christ can cast out all demons and sins, regardless of their nature or origin.

But before the initial reaction, we would do well to remove ourselves, as much as is possible, even from those initial stirrings, by avoiding the near occasions of sins of lust, wherever they may lurk in our lives. Are there activities or places we would be wise to avoid altogether in order to withdraw ourselves from lust's battlefield?

Prayer for Peace between Body and Soul

So great is our need for grace beyond nature in conquering lust that we have already touched just a bit upon prayer in our earlier battle-plan sections. The prayer that Christ gave us is also a powerful weapon against lust and her lusty daughters. Christ bids us to pray, "Lead us not into temptation, but deliver us from evil." Because of lust's powerful "quickstep" action, this petition is especially relevant to temptations toward lust. When we ask God to help us stay clear of temptations, we must be mindful of what we ask and willing to do our part to walk our prayer talk, to line up the actions of our feet with those of our lips and literally to walk away from evils that will tempt us.

Temperance Tames Lust

Temperance is the cardinal virtue that controls our desires for concupiscible pleasures, and chastity is its specific allied virtue that takes on the battles of lust. The very mention of chastity may call to the minds of some an age-old weapon in the war against lust, that of "chastity of the eyes." This idea again gets at lust's swift movements within the soul and seeks to nip them in the bud. We are all called to the chastity consistent with our state in life, whether we are married or not, and by practicing chastity of the eyes we will help God help "deliver us from evil."

First, we must train ourselves not to seek out images that will entice us to lust, be they virtual images on the computer screen, on the television, or on the movie screen, or real-live images on the beach, at the gym, walking down the street, or indeed, even in church.

Second, when we do encounter the image of a beautiful body, whether or not the person's clothing is inappropriate for the setting, we need to recall that that person's *body* is indeed the body of a *person*. St. Thomas himself advised that "the most effective remedy against intemperance is not to dwell on the consideration of singulars."[77] No God-fearing person wants to be intemperate, unchaste, or lustful in general, but is drawn down that path by particular, individual lures to pleasure.

St. Thomas would suggest that we focus on the opposite of those "singulars," namely, "universals." For instance, a man, instead of turning his eyes and imagination on this or that particular woman, can try focusing on "woman." Instead of lusting after a particular woman, he can try focusing on her identity as a daughter or a sister, and perhaps as someone else's current or future wife or mother. Instead of emulating the Don Juan-like "lover" who lusts after women but does not really love them at all, he can emulate the man who shows true love for women by honoring and respecting them.

Spouses blessed with the sacrament of marriage can treat each other with special loving attention as singulars. Indeed, St. Thomas wrote about the appropriateness of a wife adorning herself and striving to make herself attractive to her husband, and there is no reason husbands should not seek to make themselves attractive to their wives. Yet, the married couple, too, should strive to love rather than to lust, loving each other in the flesh, yet never seeing or using the other as mere flesh alone.

Passionate Pursuit of Pure Pleasure

St. Thomas was especially adept at practicing temperance because of his focus on the very highest of universals, the divine things of God. Spiritual sloth, as we saw earlier, paves the way for lust and

---

[77] *ST*, II-II, Q. 142, art. 3.

intemperance because "those who find no joy in spiritual things have recourse to pleasures of the body."[78] To curb lust then, let us focus most on the highest things of God, from which love, not lust, will flow. Spiritual pleasures then are the "pure" pleasures of which we speak. When we are pure of heart we are in the best position to see God. When we strive to see God and to guide our lives by His light, we are in the best position to keep our hearts and bodies pure.

Christ Embodies Love over Lust

" 'Woman, behold, your son! Then he said to the disciple, 'Behold, your mother!' " (John 19:26–27). These are last words of Christ that Archbishop Fulton Sheen said served as reparation for the world's sins of lust. In His death on the Cross, "in reparation for all the sins of the flesh, He is almost disposed of His flesh, for according to Sacred Scripture the very bones of his body could be numbered."[79] Christ, who had no sin, gave up all worldly attachments, including His own mother and His own flesh, for our sake.

Christ was made incarnate through the Virgin Mary and received no taint of Original Sin. Blessed Mary herself was graced by God with an immaculate conception and bore no stain of original or acquired sin, and yet both willingly suffered greatly from and for the sins of others. Neither of them sinned with lust, although their hearts went out to those who suffered from the vice of lust. Christ dined with prostitutes and forgave the adulteress, although he bid them to forgo their sinful ways in order to follow him who is the true way. Unlike the others, including Judas Iscariot, He did not chide the sinful woman Mary

[78] *ST*, II-II, Q. 35. art. 4.
[79] *The Seven Capital Sins*, p. 29.

of Bethany, who anointed his feet with her precious perfume. Instead He said she had done a beautiful thing, and He blessed and praised her (cf. John 12:1–8).

When we are tempted by those first stirrings of lust, we must admit our weakness and call out to God for help, and let us specifically call out as well for the help of His Son and for His Holy Mother. They will help us conquer lust, and if we should turn from their help and be conquered instead, they will ever stand ready to return us to our feet, dust us off, and re-arm us with temperance and chastity to reenter the fray.

CHAPTER 14

Routing Wrath

But anger may be routed by precepts;
for it is a weakness of the mind
that is subject to the will.

—SENECA[80]

---

[80] Seneca, *Moral Essays*, vol. 1, trans. John W. Basore (Cambridge, MA: Harvard University Press), *On Anger*, bk. 2, chap. 1, 169.

Are You Riled Up Enough to Take Anger to Task?

We saw that wrath, or excessive anger, is also a very powerful and deadly sin, because it, like lust, builds on a natural sensitive passion hardwired into our fallen human nature. Whereas lust is a failure of our reason to rein in our concuspicible appetite for things that we desire, wrath is a failure of our reason to rein in our irascible appetite that seeks to fight back against things that thwart our desires. "Nature does nothing without a purpose," per Aristotle. Our concuspicible, fleshly desires ensure the propagation of our species, and those irascible, fight-or-flight responses ensure our safety and survival. We've seen as well that part of the reason the seven capital vices are so deadly is that they seek out things that seem good to us, and when we have chosen the wrong goods to seek, we let loose legions of sinful behaviors that serve these ill-chosen ends.

Still, wrath, like all the capital vices or deadly sins, has chinks in its armor that reason can help penetrate, especially when aided by divine assistance. To paraphrase the Stoic Seneca, who literally wrote the book on anger, anger is a weakness of the mind that our will can indeed "route by precepts." Let's check out some routes to that route and the precepts with which we may arm ourselves.

Rooting Out Wrath

To examine your conscience for the vice of wrath, you might want to start by examining your *heart*—the real, fist-size one residing under your sternum. We see Thomas's integrated view of matter and spirit, body and soul, most clearly in his treatment of the passion of anger. He notes that some describe anger as "a kindling of blood around the heart," that "a disposition to anger arises from an emotion of the soul due to the wrong inflicted."[81] It's interesting that he touches on anger's connection with the heart, given that some modern research on people with the driven, type-A personality indicates that those most prone to heart attacks have a tendency toward frequent bouts of anger.

So then, to reflect on your possible recent sins of wrath, you might begin by asking yourself whether you have felt riled up by anything lately. Has anything gotten your heart pounding, raised your blood pressure, and spurred thoughts of revenge? If so, has it clouded or partially blinded your reason? Has it tempted you to acts of injustice? Recalling that Thomas and Aristotle, unlike some of the most stalwart of Stoic philosophers, wrote that anger is not always a sin, you might ask yourself, if you were so riled up, was your anger directed at the right person (a truly guilty party), at the right time (after a delay for cooling and reflection), and for the right reasons (to avenge a true wrong and to correct the guilty party rather than to harm him)?

Have you become an angry person in one of the three ways described by Aristotle, St. Gregory of Nyssa, and St. John Damascene? You might ask yourself questions like these:

---

[81] *ST*, I-II, Q. 22, art. 2; Q. 46, arts. 5, 6.

- Have I allowed myself to become *choleric* and irritable, with a hair-triggered anger that goes off at the slightest of inconveniences? Have I cursed the driver who drove too slowly, the cabinet that got in the way of my head, or the bedpost that crashed into my toe?

- Have I allowed myself to become *sullen*, nursing old wounds, keeping them locked in my chest, perhaps even relishing my slowly seething and simmering anger, making sure its coals stay lit until I am able to obtain revenge?

- Have I become so *ill-tempered*, *stern*, or *rancorous* that I have not relented in my anger or apologized even after I have taken out some unjust action of revenge or punishment, perhaps even with a loved one?

We might search our consciences as well for wrath's half-dozen death-dealing daughters:

- Have my thoughts been enkindled by wrath? Have I mentally belittled the object of my anger, denigrating his worth through the daughter of *indignation*? Have I experienced *swelling of mind*, as my calm and rational thoughts have been overwhelmed by growing thoughts of revenge?

- Have my words been wrathful? Has my anger led to the confused, thoughtless, or vulgar words that bespeak *clamor*? Have I purposely insulted and reviled someone with words that bespeak *contumely*? Have I been so carried away with rage that I have even cursed God Himself with words bespeaking *blasphemy*?

- Have my actions been wrathful? Have I engaged in *quarreling*, angrily provoking others and possibly leading to hurtful acts, even acts of violence?

Confession Confounds Wrath

Having examined our conscience for traces of wrathful thoughts, words, and deeds, we are in the best position to work to eradicate such sins in the future and to obtain forgiveness for past sins of wrath. Wrathful anger is dangerous because it can so easily cloud and even blind our reason. To confess sins of wrath, on the contrary, demands the use of our reason, to put those wrathful sins under reason's microscope, after our heart rates and thought rates have returned to baseline. If we can train ourselves to cull out and confess the various kinds and daughters of wrath that we may tend to manifest the most often, our confessor will be in the best possible position to help supply us with remedies to wrath from his own priestly experience.

The holy sacrament of the Eucharist can also aid us in the war against wrath. St. Thomas carefully examined the verses of Matthew 5:21–22, in which Christ warns us of the penalties against wrathful words and deeds against one's brother. In the very next two verses, Christ tells us that if we go to offer a gift at that altar and we remember that our brother has something against us, we must hurry to be reconciled with him before we offer our gift. Recalling that we are all brothers in Christ through Baptism and that Christ instituted the sacrament of Reconciliation,[82] it is very clear that we should seek to be reconciled with all who have been harmed by our wrath before we go to the altar, not only to offer a gift, but to receive that ultimate gift that Christ

[82] Matt. 16:19; John 20:23.

gives us of His own Body and Blood, soul and divinity, under the appearance of bread and wine.

Stepping Away from Wrath Is as Easy as ABC

The steps of the vice and sin wrath can follow quickly upon the passion of natural anger. To see this in action, let's imagine one small and painful misstep. Let's say a huge man steps on your foot as he passes by you in a crowded bus, and without a word of apology. Might you be angry? It seems like a clear-cut case of the old stimulus-response (S-R) psychology. The stimulus (S) of the huge man's stepping on your foot has immediately produced the response (R) of your pain and anger. After all, haven't you frequently told people, "*You* made me angry!" Actually, though, modern cognitive psychologists have pointed out that something actually does go on between the S and the R. They label this the O, for organism. Our minds are not empty, black boxes. Something goes on inside us between the big guy's heel, our painful foot, and our angry reaction, between someone's hurtful action and our angry response.

Modern cognitive psychologists, such as Rational-Emotive Behavior Therapy founder Albert Ellis, have borrowed ideas from Stoics such as Epictetus and Seneca (so well known to St. Thomas), and have rearranged the alphabet in a very simple way to explain our emotional reactions to outside events. To make it as easy as ABC, the stimulus (S) becomes the activating event (A), the response (R) becomes the emotional or behavioral consequence (C), and the organism (O) is refined and renamed belief (B), because that is the main thing that goes on in our minds between the external event and our own reactions. Abstract enough? Then let's make it as simple as ABC by reframing our little scenario a bit.

The ABCs of

A	B	C
Activating event	*Beliefs (irrational)*	*Emotional consequence*
Big guy steps on foot. (He is blind.)	"The careless oaf should watch his step! I'd like to get even with him."	Anger
Big guy steps on foot. (He is not blind; he does this on purpose.)	"The careless oaf should watch his step! I'd like to get even with him."	Anger

Let's say that a huge man steps on your foot as he passes you in a crowded bus without a word of apology (A). Might you be angry (C)? It is time to call in the (B), for it is *beliefs* that can serve to conquer our own excessive anger. What if you then noticed the man's dark glasses and white cane? Your foot might still hurt like the dickens, but would you still be *angry* with him? Chances are you would not, because your belief about him would have changed. You would no longer tell yourself what a knave he is but might tell yourself how noble he is to get out and travel alone despite his blindness, praying that God might give you such grace were you in the same position.

Modern systems of psychotherapy and ancient Stoic philosophical techniques go much deeper than this, though, in their remedies against anger. What if that big dude was not blind and actually enjoys crunching people's toes? Must we still feel angry at him and upset ourselves over his action? More accurately stated, must we *make ourselves* angry and upset? Ellis and

Emotional Disturbance

D	E
Disputation of Beliefs leading to new, rational beliefs	*New emotional consequence*
"He's blind. It was an accident. How courageous for him to travel alone."	Forgiveness and admiration
"What a sorry thing for a grown man to think that is appropriate. I'll pray for him. My painful foot is not very much compared with Christ's pain on the Cross."	Forgiveness and compassion, along with reasonable annoyance

Seneca would emphatically answer, "No!" Although Aristotle and Aquinas acknowledge times when anger can be just, they too would champion the use of our reason to form reasonable beliefs that may detonate most angry reactions. These beliefs are among the "precepts" that Seneca states can "route" anger. When we get angry, we tend to rile ourselves up further in our self-talk, ruminating on our pain and the injustice of whatever kind of insult we believed we have suffered.

The use of our faculty of reason to rein in emotions such as anger adds another letter to our alphabetic arsenal, namely, D, for disputation of beliefs. When we dispute automatic beliefs that produce anger in our souls, we may then go on to exchange a sinful C for a virtuous new E (emotional consequence). The chart above lays all this out simply for our little example:

Methods like these can be used to help us keep anger at the lowest steps of the ladder that leads to the sin of wrath, if we keep precepts like these in mind:

- *Delay*: The first thing to do when some activating event (A) has occurred and you realize you feel angry and desire to seek vengeance or punishment on someone (C) is to *delay* taking action. This is embodied in the simple, homespun, but effective advice to count to ten when angry and to avoid taking action until you've calmed down.

- *Dispute*: Next, call in the D! Delaying provides us the time to let our cool, rational mind take over from our boiling heart so that we may *dispute* those anger-producing beliefs, those things we tell ourselves that fuel our anger and desire for revenge. We might try to see the issue through our offender's eyes and give him the benefit of the doubt regarding his motives for whatever action we have perceived as an insult. This may help produce a new, more rational belief and a calmer emotional reaction (E).

- *Inoculate* yourself against further bouts of anger by preparing for them and forgiving your transgressors in advance. The Stoic emperor Marcus Aurelius advised that every morning on arising, we should remind ourselves that we are going to encounter "the busybody, the thankless, the overbearing, the treacherous, the envious, the unneighborly,"[83] and this rings as true in our day as it did in the second century. Aurelius elaborated that some people act this way because they do not truly understand good and evil, and that *our* souls cannot be

---

[83] Marcus Aurelius, *Meditations* (Cambridge, MA: Harvard University Press), 305.

debased by *their* actions. Further, if we do understand the good, we will understand that they share with us the same humanity and reason and that we cannot hate them, but must value them as kinsmen, placed in the world for cooperation, and not for resentment and aversion. These are good Stoic suggestions that good Christians who wish to avoid wrath should endorse and practice daily!

As We Forgive Those Who Trespass against Us

The advice Aurelius gave for inoculating ourselves against anger may call to mind petitions from the prayer that Christ himself gave us: "Forgive us our trespasses, as we forgive those who trespass against us." In praying the Lord's Prayer we are not only putting Aurelius's sage advice into practice, but asking God to assist us in the process. If we ponder these words we will recall our own tendencies toward sin (including, of course, the seven deadly ones!) and how our actions may, either intentionally or inadvertently, harm others and promote their anger. We pray that through God's grace we ourselves may not be nosy, thankless, treacherous, overbearing, unneighborly blokes who prompt our neighbor's wrath! We also pledge to God that we will forgive those who harm or insult us in some way, promising, in effect, that we will work to dispute and to conquer the capital vice of wrath, in all its manifestations, and in all of its death-dealing daughters.

The Placating Powers of Patience, Clemency, and Meekness

As powerful and unruly as the vice of wrath and its daughters can be, we should be sure to arm ourselves with three calm but powerful virtues that can put them in their place. *Patientia* (patience) is a virtue related to fortitude that St. Thomas tells us enables us to endure hardships and suffering without becoming sorrowful or defeated, especially when these hardships have been produced by the actions of others. If you've ever heard someone told, "You have the patience of a saint," chances are the saint-like one has kept cool and endured with calmness and grace the annoying and bothersome behavior of another person—perhaps complaints, disrespect, or ingratitude from someone he was trying to help. If we think about the calm, cool, saint-like virtue of patience and actively strive to cultivate it in our thoughts, words, and deeds, our souls will house much less space for wrath.

Sometimes justice might call for some kind of punishment of a transgressor, and here we may call forth the virtue of *clementia* (clemency). Clemency is related to the cardinal virtue of temperance, and it tempers our desire for revenge. Per Thomas, "through the passion of anger a man is provoked to inflict a too severe punishment, while it belongs directly to clemency to mitigate punishment, and this might be prevented by excess anger."[84] In the same article, Thomas notes that, according to Seneca, "clemency is a leniency of a superior toward an inferior."

Of historical interest, Seneca once wrote an entire essay on the virtue of clemency (*De Clementia*) hoping to inspire with this virtue, so well-aligned with Christian teaching, the son of one Lucius Domitius Ahenobarbus, a young man to whom he served as adviser. The young man could not have rejected Seneca's advice more completely, becoming one of the world's greatest examples of a man who chose wrathful and cruel punishment

[84] *ST,* II-II, Q. 157, art. 1.

over any semblance of clemency. Indeed, he one day ordered Seneca himself to commit suicide. Countless Christian martyrs also attest to his lack of clemency, for we know that young man by his name of Nero Caesar.

Of practical importance today, although I am certain there are no Roman emperors among my readers, we all at times assume the role of superior over an inferior, whether it be in the role of a boss, a parent, a grandparent, an older sibling, a teacher, a pastor, a coach, or whatever our position of authority may be. And whatever that role may be, when wrongs have been committed and punishment of some kind is needed, we need to strive to display that noble virtue of *clementia* so the wrongdoer may not grow wrathful at our own excess but may be inspired to reform the behaviors that provoke the punishment and to be clement toward others when he may come to play the role of a punisher.

A third great virtue that works with *patientia* and *clementia* in conquering wrath and its daughters is the often misunderstood, most manly virtue of *mansuetudo* (meekness). Per Thomas, clemency and meekness may work together as they constrain "the onslaught of anger," but they differ from each other "inasmuch as clemency moderates external punishment, while meekness properly mitigates the passion of anger."

In our day, meekness may also connote weakness. We'll dispel this confusion in just a page or so, when we examine the meekness of Christ.

Erecting a Spiritual Defense against Wrath

Temptations to wrath truly embroil us within a battle of body and soul. Its bodily manifestations are so clear in the rapid beating of the heart, the clenching of the fists, the flushing of the face and scowling of the mein,[85] but we should recall that these bodily changes reflect a stirring of the "sensitive soul," those powers of sensation and emotion that we share with the animals. Unlike the animals, however, we possess "intellectual souls" that also possess the powers of reason and will. While we can be stirred by our passions, it is potentially up to our reason whether we choose to accelerate the stirring like an electric egg beater or to work to pull out the plug. Our reason and our will are spiritual powers, and through them we are made in the image and likeness of God. When we train ourselves in taming the rages of wrath with the use of cool reason and a trained will, we become more attuned to the world of the spirit and less easily conquered by the stirrings of the flesh.

The Most Manly Meekness of the Messiah

Of the seven last words of Christ, Sheen tells us the first of them were spoken in reparation for sins of wrath. "Father, forgive them, for they know not what they do" (Luke 23:34). Here is the crucified Christ, the victim of unspeakable anger, cruelty, and brutality, echoing the words that He taught us to pray, asking God the Father to forgive those who trespass against us. Clearly then He shows us that when we are wronged, we must ask God to forgive our transgressors, rather than to seethe in rage, while plotting our revenge. This is not to say that there cannot be justifiable anger. Indeed, Christ Himself embodied such anger

[85] Indeed, some, including Seneca, have recommended merely looking in the mirror while angry as one defense against this vice, for it's not a very pretty look, and it doesn't make one look very sane! (Perhaps some readers will recall their mother warning them that their face could get stuck that way too.)

in the cleansing of the Temple (cf. John 2:13–17), and He did so in a perfect display of the virtue of meekness.

Meekness is not weakness. There are times when bold actions may be required, but even just anger must be moderated in how it is experienced and displayed. Christ overturned the tables and expressed words of chastisement at the moneychangers who debased the house of his Father, but He did not turn them into dust. He hated the sin but loved the sinners, moderating His anger always, and most amazingly so as He willingly suffered His death on the Cross—and what clemency did He show! Clemency, you'll recall, entails leniency of a superior toward an inferior. Who could be more superior to us all than God incarnate Himself? Who could suffer a more unjust and heinous punishment and yet offer His punishers not pain and death but an eternal life of joy with Him if we should change our hearts, turn to Him, and live the life of love that He showed us? Who then are we to boil over in anger when a driver cuts us off, when a friend seems to snub us, when a person we help shows us no gratitude, when a big person steps on our toe, or even if we should stub one of our own toes? We would be much more blessed if we strove to become meek; in fact, we'd inherit the earth (cf. Matt. 5:5).

How the Mother of the Virtues Dethrones the Queen of the Vices

And so charity, that is, love of God, governs all other virtues. And so charity, although it is a special virtue if we should consider its proper object, is nonetheless common to all the virtues by reason of the diffusion of its governance. And so we call charity the form and mother of all the virtues.

And likewise, pride, although it is a special kind of sin by reason of its proper object, is nonetheless a sin common to all sins by reason of the diffusion of its governance. And so also we call pride the root and queen of all sins.

—ST. THOMAS AQUINAS, *DE MALO*, Q. 8, ART. 2

Presenting the Deadliest Sin in the World

Having gotten to know the seven deadly sins and their forty-four death-dealing daughters, now it is time to answer the question that we started with in this book: What is the deadliest sin in the world? St. Thomas, following St. Gregory the Great, argued that one sin was in a sense the deadliest of all, more prone to generate other sins, more directly opposed to the goodness of God than even the capital seven. All of the deadly sins have this sin in common, if not as their direct cause, then as an indirect consequence. The sin that has pride of place is the sin of *pride* itself.

The Queen of the Vices

All sins involve a turning toward some lesser good or pleasure, while turning away from higher goods and, ultimately, from God. Some sins may be committed through ignorance or weakness, and may not be directly intended as affronts to God. Pride does not necessarily engender every sin one commits, but it has the potential to spawn every form of sin. A person may have serious problems with lust or with wrath, for example, but realize they offend God and strive mightily to conquer them. A person filled with the vice of pride may feel no compunction and openly defy God in his sinful acts. The word for pride in Latin is *superbia*, and Thomas says it "is so-called because a man thereby aims higher (*supra*) than he is."[86] Pride is an inordinate desire for one's own excellence and to have things one's own way, rather than God's way.

Pride has been with us since Adam and Eve chose to follow their desires, rather than the will of God. The seven deadly sins have been with us always since that time and have always represented a spiritual struggle. Today, though, pride is attaining a very powerful ascendancy where formerly Christian cultures are becoming increasingly secularized. Man is, in essence, increasingly consciously choosing himself over God, enthroning his own will, and casting God aside as irrelevant or nonexistent.

Lust, for example, deriving from our natural desires for the procreation of the species, has been with us always and has always required struggle and restraint. But now, as never before, popular culture and media, and indeed, even some Christian religious denominations, glorify lust and strive to promote and sell every form of sexual sin as a proper expression of our sexuality, regardless of the damage to countless families and to the destruction of millions of unborn children through the abortion industry that profits from sins against chastity by charging fees for violations of the Fifth Commandment. Ignorance and weakness certainly play a role here, which is why young would-be mothers and fathers facing an unexpected pregnancy need to be educated, supported, loved, and shown the value of every life. Their ignorance and weakness would not result in a death, however, if it were not for the educated and powerful providers of abortion who willfully decide that they, and not God, are the arbiters of the value of a human life, or lack thereof. The whole

---

[86] *ST*, II-II, Q. 162, art. 1.

modern culture of death, as Pope St. John Paul II called it, could not survive without the pride of its promoters and profiteers.

Any of the seven deadly sins becomes far more deadly when openly flaunted through pride. Pride is also especially deadly because even the *virtues* that we develop may be kindling for its fires. St. Gregory described a type of pride wherein we boast of goods or virtues *we don't really have*, but he also described three types of pride that build upon good qualities we may actually possess. There is a pride of arrogance in which we think that our good comes *from ourselves*, rather than from God. There is also a pride in which we may acknowledge that our good comes from God, but we believe *we have earned it due to our own merits*. Yet another kind of pride "*despises others and wish[es] to appear the exclusive possessors of what they have.*"[87]

We must exercise special care, even as we pursue virtue, so that we do not fail to acknowledge our gratitude to God for whatever success we may achieve. Pride may lurk within even apparently quite saintly souls, and we must all exercise care that it does not lead us to a fall.

Catholic psychologist Henri Joly (1839–1925) tells the story of two would-be saints who stumbled through simple acts of pride. St. Philip Neri had been sent by the pope to visit a monastery to interview a sister who had reportedly been blessed with private revelations and ecstasies. Philip headed out for the monastery on his mule on a very stormy night. When he arrived and the sister was brought before him, "she appeared full of sweetness and unction."[88] Philip then sat down, stuck out his leg, and said

---

[87] *ST*, II-II, Q. 162, art. 4.
[88] Henri Joly, *The Psychology of the Saints* (Fort Collins, CO: Roman Catholic Books, n.d.), 58.

to her, "Pull off my boots." Upon seeing the sister draw herself up, disdainful and clearly scandalized, he had seen all he needed to see. "He seized his hat and went back to the Vatican, to tell the Holy Father that a religious, so devoid of humility, could not possibly possess the graces and virtues she was credited with."[89] The key word there is *humility*.

Joly tells of a similar incident in which a priest was called to examine another young woman supposedly blessed with extraordinary graces. "'You are the saint, aren't you?' he said to her. 'Yes, Father,' was the answer he got. The illusion was instantly detected."[90]

True humility is the bane of pride, and it is shown by real saints. When someone once told St. Thérèse of Lisieux that she was a saint, she rejoined, "No, I am not a saint. I am a very little soul whom God has overwhelmed with graces. In heaven you will see that I am speaking the truth."

Humility then is the virtue especially opposed to pride. Especially attentive and retentive readers will recall that we addressed humility briefly in chapter 9 on ending envy. Humility counteracts the envy that springs from that type of pride that Gregory said, as we saw above, "despises others and wish[es] to appear the exclusive possessors of what they have." Humility opposes all forms of pride. It grounds us in the earth and reminds us who we are and where we come from.

In his book *The Theological Virtues*, the learned twentieth-century Dominican theologian Fr. Réginald Garrigou-Lagrange provided a wonderful graphic image depicting the relationship

[89] Joly, *The Psychology of the Saints*, 58.
[90] Ibid., 58, fn.

between Christian virtues.[91] Christ is the rock upon which the structure is built. The hinges of its doors are the cardinal virtues of prudence, justice, fortitude, and temperance (since *cardo* is Latin for "hinge"), and on the doors are written the names of other associated virtues and gifts of the Holy Spirit. The base that sits on the rock on which the rest of the edifice stands is the virtue of humility. If we are not humble, we will succumb to pride, and our edifice of virtue will crumble. The structure is crowned by an arch, and the left and right pillars are marked "faith" and "hope." Which virtue stands at its pinnacle at the top of the arch? Well, faith and hope are theological virtues, and we know from St. Paul (1 Cor. 13:13) that faith and hope abide with one other virtue, and it is the greatest of all. It is the mother of the virtues and the greatest antidote to pride and to all manner of deadly sins.

The Mother of the Virtues

St. Thomas wrote a great deal about sin because he knew there were so many ways we can miss the mark. There are so many false, partial, and changeable goods that can distract our pursuit of the true, complete, and unchangeable goods that God would have us enjoy. Yet, as we have seen, he was not nearly so interested in how low we can go as in how high we can rise. For this reason, he wrote far more on virtue than he did on sin. And what is the highest virtue to which we can rise? It is the love that is *charity*. Thomas calls charity the mother of all the virtues, since "every virtue depends on it in a way."[92] All the moral virtues depend

---

[91] TAN Books was so gracious as to allow me to duplicate it in my own *Three Irish Saints* (Charlotte, NC: TAN Books, 2011), 188.

[92] *ST*, II-II, Q. 23, art. 4.

on the practical wisdom of prudence to select the right *means* to their ends, but how do we know if the ends that we seek are truly virtuous? We know if they align with *ordo caritatis*, the order of charity. When Jesus summed up the law and the commandments to tell us to love God with all our hearts and our neighbor as ourselves, He commanded us to live the life of charity. God is the most virtuous, highest, and last of all ends. Charity resides in the will, and the will desires, seeks, and loves the good. The love of charity seeks the highest good, union with God.

Thomas says that the chief act of charity is to love, and, as we have seen, he compares the love of charity to the heat of a powerful furnace.[93] The stronger the furnace of charity we build within ourselves, the further will its flames reach, serving even to heat strangers and our enemies. But since those closest to the furnace should get the most heat, true charity should begin at home and be directed in the greatest intensity toward those with whom we live out our daily lives.

When we are aflame with the love of charity, pride and the capital vices may well go up in smoke. Pride and capital sins, the foundations and pillars of vice, say, "me, myself, and I." Humility and charity, the base and the pinnacle of virtue, the left and right bookends of the books of virtue, say "God, neighbor, and *then* yes, me too."

All manner of vices grow in strength and magnitude from repeated sinful acts, but we should recall that virtue grows too from simple daily deeds. Aristotle said we become builders by building and harpists by playing the harp. St. Thomas tells us that each loving act of charity we perform increases within us the tendency to perform more charitable acts, "and this readiness

---

[93] *ST,* II-II, Q. 27, art. 7.

increasing, man breaks out into an act of more fervent love, and strives to advance in charity, and then his charity increases actually."[94]

If we are to defeat pride, sloth, envy, avarice, vainglory, gluttony, wrath, lust, and all of their sundry death-dealing daughters, we must turn to God and ask Him to bless us with the mother of the virtues and with all of her sturdy sons and virtuous daughters. We must practice them every day, and show our children, friends, and neighbors, by our words and deeds, that virtue can prevail over all manner of vice, and all from the grace and for the glory of God.

[94] *ST*, II-II, Q. 24, art. 6.

Wicked Words: A Brief History of the Names of the Seven Deadly Sins

Wicked Word #1: Sloth

The word for the capital vice of *sloth* has roots in the transliterated Hebrew word *atsel*, denoting a lazy person or sluggard. Its use in the Christian tradition of the seven deadly sins appears as *akedia*, from the Greek denoting boredom or apathy, particularly a spiritual boredom or apathy, rather than merely laziness or indolence that avoids physical exertion. The Latinized version is *acedia*, as appears in the *Summa Theologica*. Most English translations use the word *sloth*. The *Catechism of the Catholic Church* lists it as "sloth or acedia" (no. 1866).

Wicked Word #2: Envy

The word for the capital vice of *envy* comes from the transliterated Hebrew word *qana*, meaning jealousy or envy. It does not appear in the earliest Christian writings of the Greek Fathers that led to the list of the seven deadly sins but was added by St. Gregory the Great. He used the Latin word *invidia*, which comes from the word *invidere*, "to look upon." This is the word St. Thomas used for the vice in the *Summa Theologica*. English translations and the *Catechism* (no. 1866) use the word *envy*.

Wicked Word #3: Avarice

The word for the capital vice of *avarice* comes from various Hebrew words, such as *havah*, meaning destructive desire or greed. In the early Christian writings of the Greek Fathers, it appears as *philarguria*, meaning love of money (literally, love of silver—*argyros*). The *Catechism* (no. 1866) lists this sin as *avarice*, deriving from the Latin *avaritia*, based on the word *avere*, meaning to desire, covet, or crave. St. Thomas uses the word *avaritia*, and in the English Dominican Fathers' translation of the *Summa Theologica*, it appears as *covetousness*.

Wicked Word #4: Vainglory

The word for the capital vice of *vainglory* has links to the Hebrew word *kavod* for honor or glory. In the writings of the early Greek Fathers it appears as *kenodoxia*, meaning empty pride or vain glory. It appears in St. Thomas's Latin as *inanis gloria*, meaning inane, empty, or vain glory. Vainglory was included in the early Greek Fathers' lists of deadly sins, and in the lists of Sts. Gregory and Thomas. The *Catechism* (no. 1866), as noted in this book's text, lists *pride*, rather than *vainglory*, among the seven deadly sins.

Wicked Word #5: Gluttony

The word for the capital vice of *gluttony* comes from the Hebrew word *zalal*, meaning to shake out or pour lavishly. In the writings of the early Greek Fathers it appears as *gastrimargia*, meaning a madness of the gut or stomach. It appears in St. Thomas's Latin as *gula*, deriving from the word meaning to swallow. The *Catechism* (no. 1866) lists the sin of *gluttony* among the seven deadly sins.

Wicked Word #6: Lust

The word for the capital vice of *lust* comes from the Hebrew word *agabah* for inordinate love. In the writings of the early

Greek Father Evagrius it appears as *porneia*, meaning desire for fornication or other forms of sexual immorality. It appears in St. Thomas's Latin as *luxuria*, deriving from the Latin word for excess or extravagance as applied to sexual desires. The *Catechism* (no. 1866) lists *lust* among the seven deadly sins.

Wicked Word #7: Wrath

The word for the capital vice of *wrath* has links to the Hebrew word *aph* for anger and is sometimes found with the word *charah* for burning, yielding "burning anger." In the writings of the early Greek Fathers it appears as *orge*, meaning an internal swelling of anger. It appears in St. Thomas's Latin as *ira*, the Latin word for anger. The Dominican Fathers' translated *ira* in the *Summa Theologica* as "anger," and we see its survival in the English word *ire*, meaning intense anger. The *Catechism of the Catholic Church* (no. 1866) translates *ira* as "wrath" in its list of deadly sins. *Wrath* is also used in this book as a reminder of the distinction between the natural human passion of *anger* and the sin of *excessive, inordinate anger*.

Christ's Seven Last Words on the Cross and the Seven Deadly Sins[95]

Christ's Last Words	Corresponding Deadly Sin
"Father, forgive them; for they know not what they do." (Luke 23:34)	Anger (wrath)
"Truly, I say to you, today you will be with me in Paradise." (Luke 23:43)	Envy
"Woman, behold, your son!...Behold, your mother!" (John 19:26–27)	Lust
"My God, my God, why hast thou forsaken me?"(Matt. 27:46; Mark 15:34)	Pride
"I thirst." (John 19:28)	Gluttony
"It is finished." (John 19:30)	Sloth
"Father, into thy hands I commit my spirit!" (Luke 23:46)	Avarice

[95] See Fulton J. Sheen, *The Seven Capital Sins* (New York: Alba House, 2001).

A Traditional Master Chart of Vices, Virtues, and Vice Versa

Seven Deadly Sins	Seven Contrary Virtues
Pride	Humility
Avarice	Charity
Envy	Kindness
Wrath	Patience
Lust	Chastity
Gluttony	Temperance
Sloth or Acedia	Diligence

The Seven Capital Vices and Their Forty-Four

Sloth II-II, 35, 4	Envy II-II, 36, 4	Avarice II-II, 118, 8	Vainglory II-II,132, 5
Malice	Hatred	Treachery	Disobedience
Spite	Tale-bearing	Fraud	Boastfulness
Faintheartedness	Detraction	Falsehood	Hypocrisy
Despair	Joy at another's misfortune	Perjury	Contention
Sluggish-ness about the Commandments	Grief at another's prosperity	Restlessness	Obstinacy
Wandering of the mind after unlawful things		Violence	Discord
		Insensitivity to mercy	Eccentricity

* This chart also appears in chapter 7 of this book and is presented again here for ease of reference in examining one's conscience.

Death-Dealing Daughters in the *Summa Theologica**

Gluttony	Lust	Wrath
II-II, 148, 6	II-II, 153, 5	II-II, 158, 8
Unseemly joy	Blindness of mind	Quarreling
Scurrility	Thoughtlessness	Swelling of the mind
Uncleanness	Inconstancy	Contumely
Loquaciousness	Rashness	Clamor
Dullness of mind	Self-love	Indignation
	Hatred of God	Blasphemy
	Love of the world	
	Abhorrence and despair of a future world	

Kevin Vost

Kevin Vost (b. 1961) holds a Doctor of Psychology in Clinical Psychology (Psy.D.) degree from the Adler School of Professional Psychology in Chicago. He has taught at Aquinas College in Nashville, the University of Illinois at Springfield, MacMurray College, and Lincoln Land Community College. He has served as a research review committee member for American Mensa, a society promoting the scientific study of human intelligence, and as an advisory board member for the International Association of Resistance Trainers, an organization that certifies personal fitness trainers. Dr. Vost drinks great drafts of coffee while studying time-less, Thomistic tomes in the company of his wife, two sons, and their two dogs, in Springfield, Illinois.

Sophia Institute

Sophia Institute is a nonprofit institution that seeks to nurture the spiritual, moral, and cultural life of souls and to spread the Gospel of Christ in conformity with the authentic teachings of the Roman Catholic Church.

Sophia Institute Press fulfills this mission by offering translations, reprints, and new publications that afford readers a rich source of the enduring wisdom of mankind.

Sophia Institute also operates two popular online Catholic resources: CrisisMagazine.com and CatholicExchange.com.

Crisis Magazine provides insightful cultural analysis that arms readers with the arguments necessary for navigating the ideological and theological minefields of the day. *Catholic Exchange* provides world news from a Catholic perspective as well as daily devotionals and articles that will help you to grow in holiness and live a life consistent with the teachings of the Church.

In 2013, Sophia Institute launched Sophia Institute for Teachers to renew and rebuild Catholic culture through service to Catholic education. With the goal of nurturing the spiritual, moral, and cultural life of souls, and an abiding respect for the role and work of teachers, we strive to provide materials and programs that are at once enlightening to the mind and ennobling to the heart; faithful and complete, as well as useful and practical.

Sophia Institute gratefully recognizes the Solidarity Association for preserving and encouraging the growth of our apostolate over the course of many years. Without their generous and timely support, this book would not be in your hands.

www.SophiaInstitute.com
www.CatholicExchange.com
www.CrisisMagazine.com
www.SophiaInstituteforTeachers.org

Sophia Institute Press® is a registered trademark of Sophia Institute.
Sophia Institute is a tax-exempt institution as defined by the
Internal Revenue Code, Section 501(c)(3). Tax I.D. 22-2548708.